PLEASE STOP THE WORLD, GOD, I WANT TO GET OFF!

PLEASE STOP THE WORLD, GOD, I WANT TO GET OFF!

▼

by
Daniel C. Ball

Writers Club Press
San Jose · New York · Lincoln · Shanghai

This book is dedicated to my mother,
Norma Jean, without whom
this wonderful life would not
have been possible.

CONTENTS

Chapter 1

▼

THE WINTER OF MY DISCONTENT

I was miserable. I had just been rejected by the third girl I had asked out in the last few months. Her rejection capped off an entire year of chronic, debilitating depression. There was no end in sight to my pain.

It was May 1977, and I was completing my freshman year at the University of Portland. At 17, my life was in disarray. I was confused and didn't know what to do. I was a freshman taking courses in premed. A few members of my family were doctors, so it seemed natural for me to become a physician. But deep down inside, I really wasn't sure practicing medicine was what I wanted to do. To make matters worse, I was struggling in my classes because I couldn't concentrate enough to study.

My older friend Jerry (not his real name) had just informed me that he was graduating from college a year earlier than expected, while I was still undecided about which direction I was going to take with my life. He was moving on to veterinary school, and I was contemplating a drastic change of majors.

Jerry's face beamed with enthusiasm as he told me his other big news. "Sandra and I are getting married before the end of the year." I cringed with jealousy. Sandra had beautiful dark eyes and long, auburn hair. Jerry was lucky to be marrying such an attractive woman. I felt dejected. His news stung like salt in my emotional wounds.

It's not that my family didn't support me. My father had sold a truck to help pay for my tuition, and I knew how tough it had been for him to do this. He was very determined that I would graduate from the University of Portland, a private, religious school. My mother also was happy that I was attending the university. She had been employed there and knew that the school was highly regarded. It was more expensive than other local colleges, but they both felt the sacrifice would be worth it.

In spite of my parent's generosity, however, I was mired in debt. I had run up charges on gas cards and credit cards and was burdened with additional tuition payments, which I had borrowed money to pay for. Though I was working a long night shift and had lined up full-time work for that summer, I just couldn't make ends meet.

Driving home one evening, I fought some agonizing internal battles. I would greatly disappoint my parents if I told them I was considering changing schools to help us all save money. But how could I tell them I also was considering changing majors because I couldn't keep up academically? Up to this point I had lived a sheltered life and was still very idealistic. Plans just didn't suddenly change for me. My parents were very adamant about my future.

Now I had to figure out how to tell my parents their big dreams of my graduating from a private university and then moving on to a prestigious medical school were not going to be a reality. I had reached the end of my rope.

I pulled into the driveway of my parents' home, a large ranch house located on a 21-acre farm. I slumped my head onto the steering wheel. I didn't know what to do. I grimaced in frustration as I realized I must tell them the bad news. But how was I going to do it?

I racked my brain for the right words with which to tell my parents about my change of heart. I knew they would stew about these changes, especially my mother. I figured she wouldn't speak to me for a while.

With a deep sigh, I pushed the car door open and with lifted one heavy leg after another to the pavement. I trudged into the house and, without even a glance towards my parents, headed for my bedroom. After several minutes of pacing the floor in the darkness, I determined that now was the time to tell them. Procrastination would only intensify the growing dread I had of never being able to pursue *my* dreams.

Downcast, I headed into the room where my parents sat watching television. "Mom . . . Dad . . . I have something to tell you . . ."

*   *   *   *

I was born in Seattle to middle-class parents. My father was raised on a cattle ranch in eastern Oregon but decided he did not like ranch life. So we moved to Seattle, where my father worked at Boeing for a couple of years. Then we moved to Portland.

I remember my grade school days fondly. I attended Lynch Plaza Grade School, a small, attractive brick building offset by the wooden homes dotting a quiet Portland neighborhood.

I had some caring grade school teachers, especially Mrs. Apple. She would always place her hand on my shoulder and encourage me in whatever I was doing. She said I had tremendous capabilities. A piano teacher, Mr. Libanati, told my parents that with early and intensive training I could become a concert pianist. But I ignored this advice and hardly touched a piano.

In those years I also attended church camp often. One of the camp activities I enjoyed most was shooting BB guns. I would take aim and knock down a soup can or make holes in tin pie plates. I was getting pretty good but needed to improve my technique.

One particular Saturday afternoon, a camp counselor noticed me shooting a BB gun and offered some advice. "You have a good eye," he told me as he pushed the butt of the gun tight against my shoulder and held it steady. "But you need to concentrate more and take your time. God intends for us to succeed and do well with whatever gifts we are given, but we have to focus and work hard and ask for God's direction."

At first I shrugged off what he said. But deep inside, a seed had been planted and his words stuck with me. This was the first time that anyone who had complimented me had placed a qualification with it.

When I returned to the fifth grade that fall, I began applying myself to homework. Rather than simply waiting for good things to happen, I determined to make them happen.

The camp counselor's words began to change my life. Through the rest of grade school, junior high, and high school my grades improved to an A average and I succeeded at everything I attempted.

In high school I was happy, focused and successful at everything. I was president of the largest club in the school, the Future Farmers of America. (Estacada, my hometown, was a farming and logging community.) I was secretary of the National Honor Society, had been inducted into Who's Who among High School Students, was confirmed into Distinguished American High School Students, and invited to apply for membership in Mensa. I was a member of the Fire Club, the Key Club, the Computer Club, and the Golf Club. I was "Big Man on Campus."

With these accomplishments, I figured I would be successful no matter what I did. I was supported and encouraged by both peers and teachers. My math instructors told my parents they thought I was "going somewhere." Even one of my computer instructors mentioned that I had the talent to design whole computer systems.

*   *   *   *

My announcement stunned my mother, but my father was very understanding. Still, they weren't ready to let go of their dreams for me.

At their urging, I enrolled for my sophomore year at the University of Portland. They had convinced me to give premed one more year. I capitulated, not wanting to let on to them just how miserable I was.

During my sophomore year, my debt grew, my depression deepened, and my unhappiness with the knowledge that I wasn't doing what I wanted to do increase.

At times I became so despondent that I actually thought I would be better off dead. One night that fall I stood at the edge of the cliff overlooking the Willamette River and downtown Portland and wished I could jump off and fly away as if on the wings of eagles. But, miraculously, I never made any serious attempt at suicide.

Finally, sometime in the summer of 1978, I cried out in desperation to God, "Please help me! I don't know what to do. I can't keep going on like this. Give me some direction. Give me some hope. Restore my life. If I am supposed to die, then kill me! But please help me. Can You show me what to do?"

For what seemed like an eternity, there was no answer. Without thinking any further and beginning to believe there would be no answer, I filled a busy schedule with classes for the fall semester of my junior year.

Rather than solving my problem immediately, God gave me a vision as a life lesson, as a way to understand the meaning of pain, sorrow and human suffering. The oldest book in the Bible, Job, is all about suffering. Apart from God pain has little meaning, and those who don't know Him fight it tooth and nail. The world tries to bury its sorrows in drugs, alcohol, or suicide. But God says these are not the "outs" we should be looking for; instead, we should keep our eyes upon Him and wait for Him to provide the best resolution. This was His purpose for both my pain and the vision He gave me at the end of my sophomore year.

Chapter 2

▼

THE VISION

My class schedule for my sophomore year was full and overwhelming. As the winter wore on my depression deepened, and the rain of Portland continued to dampen my spirits. I became oblivious even to the change of seasons. I hardly noticed as the brilliant colors of fall faded into the bleak gray of winter. Days blended together in a frenzy of activity as if conspiring to keep me further behind in my studies.

Through it all I continued to read my Bible, pray for guidance, and cling to the hope that God would answer my prayer and redirect my life.

Finally, in May the sun began to break through the clouds and shine into the trees, providing the first signs of spring. I noticed my mood began to lift a bit.

One Friday morning as I awoke, I noticed the sun's warmth penetrating the late winter air. I saw the blue sky and watched the puffy, translucent clouds form and drift away. I heard birds singing as they flitted from tree to tree readying their nests for the hatching season. My blossoming elation changed into intense spiritual bliss.

To this day, I remember my strange feeling that morning. For the first time in nearly a year I smiled as the sun's brilliance brought to life every molecule of my being.

I wondered if God was beginning to answer my prayer. As I lay in bed and looked up at the ceiling, I began to see a tiny figure form. I knew immediately who this was. It was the Christ I had known intimately as a child. I began talking to Him about my problems and He understood me instantly. He empathized with my sorrow. I listened intently as His words softly yet distinctly emanated, "You will be healed. Your life will be fine." My mind became clear as I listened. "You will find happiness in life. You will find peace."

At that point, I thought, "Whew! Thank you, Lord!" For nearly a year I had been really hurting, with no relief in sight. But now I had this revelation of emotional healing. I clung to Christ's promise.

I looked up as the faint figure continued to move towards me. He was smiling. Without speaking, he lifted my mood even further until I felt an intense, indescribable happiness. At once I realized my depression was gone. As if by a miracle, the months of darkness lifted.

Suddenly, the spiritual blinders fell from my eyes, and I realized I could truly see. I felt giddy, as if I were moving into another realm¾the unseen reality of eternity.

I knew instantly I had been given a glimpse of heaven. My earthly senses became heightened. I could see better, hear more clearly, and learn incredibly fast: my mind had no limitations. On earth our senses and thought processes are dulled. In heaven they are rapidly accelerated because we have new bodies. Like the apostle Paul wrote, in this life we see through a glass dimly (1 Corinthians 13:12), but in heaven everything is opened up and is clear. Although I sensed I was still a human being living on earth, Christ was allowing me to touch and experience what life was to be like when I leave this world. I had never before (nor since) experienced this sensation.

With Christ standing in my room, I began to feel as if I were moving into the warmest part of a desert. His mere presence caused the desert to come alive: flowers bloomed, the wind calmed, and a platinum-colored lake appeared in the background, its waters rippling in the soft breeze. The temperature began to cool as if an air conditioner had been turned on.

Christ stood above me and I realized with extreme humility that He was God. He was real to me in a way that He had never been before. My doubt was gone. Just as Thomas needed to touch Christ's wounds to believe He was who He said He was, I needed this beautiful vision to restore my faith. I had given up, lost all hope, and had asked God to kill me. His response was not my physical death, but this vision.

I felt a surge of power surrounding me. He had such incredible power that with a single word He could move mountains, turn a desert into paradise, or change the world forever. He was every human's dream (and every demon's nightmare.)

I stood with mouth agape, in awe, that this glorious and powerful Being was willing to leave His kingdom for a short period of time to visit me. No words could express that moment of ecstasy. He knew my pain. He understood my plight.

The bliss I was beginning to feel was to last for three days. Much of that time I wandered around the house and the yard. My parents were gone and my sisters were at a weekend retreat. Alone, I spent my time reading, thinking, and taking long walks outside on the farm. I wanted the paradise to continue as long as it would, and at first I was afraid that the feeling would go away if I slept. But faith made it possible for me to believe that these feelings would continue as long as it was practically possible to do so.

At one point Christ turned toward me with an expression of such friendship and love that I felt overwhelmed. I had never experienced anything like this! I stared into His face for a moment as He smiled. Then I began to notice the physical details of His human form. He stood about six feet tall, with dark, shoulder-length hair and piercing eyes. He was infinitely powerful but tempered His power with infinite compassion. Without speaking, He conveyed to me a sense of glory and majesty of eternity that I will not forget. He told me, "You will have final victory. There will be struggles in your life, but you will live long on earth and build a foundation for eternity." I knew that everything on earth, in heaven, and below the earth was totally in His control and nothing could stand against His radiant power. He turned, and while motioning with His arm towards the desert, spoke His final words: "If you so choose, you may enjoy this paradise for a short while."

I glanced at the desert and then back towards Him. "But can't I have this for an eternity?" I asked.

Christ continued smiling and turned away from me. At once, a house began to materialize upon a hill. Taking a deep breath, I slowly crawled to the top where the house stood. Every move was painstaking; every rock and branch I grabbed seemed to hold me, to push me back. I had to stop and rest every few feet, as each move was so difficult. Christ had gone up to the top of the hill. I could hear His voice and could see Him wave me forward as I would stumble.

In frustrating agony I would push the branches away from me and then attempt to continue the climb around the large, jutting rocks. I tried to step over and around them, but that was too difficult. At times I simply could not step at all. My feet felt heavy, as if mired in clay. Excruciating pain seared through me as I struggled to make the next step up that hill. For hours I continued struggling, pulling myself up. The pain was unbearable.

Finally, I reached the top. Exhausted, I looked around. The walls of the house began to expand towards the plateau to the right of where I was standing. I watched as the foundation formed and the studs composing the walls went up. I stood motionless for a moment as I watched the two-by-fours and two-by-sixes form into place. Suddenly, the construction stopped. The finished walls didn't appear as I watched with silent expectation. I moved next to the magnificent frame. I looked at the floor. There was a concrete foundation beneath my feet. I examined the studs closely. They were new and bright, as if they had just come out of the kiln and been cured.

I stood silently waiting for the process to resume. For several moments it didn't.

I looked down at the floor again. I noticed puddles of water had formed on top of the concrete, indicating the newness of the foundation. Somehow I knew that the concrete foundation went deep into bedrock in the hillside. Puzzled, I looked at Christ. "Why is this home not finished?" I asked.

With a smile, He motioned me inside the house. Within moments of entering the huge foyer, my joy became so great that I could hardly stand it. "This is your home," He said. "This will be your eternal resting place." Tears streamed down my cheeks. I could not believe the happiness I felt.

"But why?" I turned to Christ and repeated my earlier question. "Why is this house not yet finished?"

"This house," Christ answered, "represents your life on earth. The climb up the hill towards the house is symbolic of your struggle on earth. There will be times of hard work, times of rejection, times of moving forward yet backward. Still, there will be times of rest and moments of happiness. The unfinished house is a symbol of accomplishment in your life on earth. If you continue to follow Me and do My will, you can achieve great things. I have laid the foundation upon which you and I together can complete this home, and it will last for an eternity."

*   *   *   *

During those three days I learned many things, most of which were lessons about my own life. But Christ also showed me that there are immutable laws that have governed the universe since its inception.

Christ gave me three promises during that time. The first was that I would be healed not only of my depression but also of my financial woes. The second was that if I continued to follow Him I would enjoy a dynamic life. I would not continue to trudge through life, fighting every step of the way, losing every battle. The third was that an eternal home in heaven awaited me, as Christ promised all His followers in John 14:2, if I continued to serve Him and others. The only true happiness on earth is found in service to both God and man.

As a sign of things to come, in an instant Christ transformed that house into a completed home.

I knew my life experience, along with its pains and sorrows, was to have eternal significance. The power and meaning of this drove deep into my spirit. I smiled and was overcome with a sense of relief. Life had meaning after all! The most powerful Being in the universe, Christ Himself, had cared enough about me to leave His kingdom for a few days to visit me and talk to me. His mere presence seemed to have sealed a wonderful future! I had no choice but to believe that this was going to happen to me.

What I saw on that hill was breathtaking: a beautiful crystal-and-white palace that looked somewhat Byzantine. The landscaped lot was immense, with the greenest grass, the most beautiful trees, and flowers in bloom. Inside, I counted dozens of rooms, each large and unique, built with different materials and employing various types of architecture. There were rooms with vaulted ceilings, rooms with curved walls, and rooms with no ceilings at all, creating views that stretched into the heavens.

With a single thought, I moved into the main room of the house. There was no front door, yet I moved into and out of the house with ease. There were no windows, yet I could see completely through the house as if the walls were made of glass. The house was like a two-way mirror. I could see outside in every direction, yet no one could see inside unless I allowed them to do so by reversing the covering on the walls. (In heaven we have the ability to be alone or not alone at any given moment. All parts of our lives are as open as we want them to be to others. We allow as much of the world to see inside our house as we choose.) I could see wide streets in the valley below and the sky that stretched into the heavens above without end. Countless stars and worlds were there to see and explore.

There was no darkness in this universe—only light. As planets and galaxies moved around one another there was merely a change in intensity of light. From a pale red-brown to indigo blue, the hues of the sky were more vast than a rainbow's.

With merely a thought, I looked back into the main room of the house, then walked into a nearby room. It was a library containing a myriad of books on history, philosophy, science, and religion. I looked at some of the titles: *The Life of Christ, History's Prophets, The Meaning of Eternity.* Each book was placed upon the shelf as if the builder had known exactly what I had been longing to know back on earth. Simply looking at the titles brought forth a rush of knowledge and emotion. In staring at the book concerning the life of Christ, I actually began experiencing His life as if I were walking in His sandals. I went back 2,000 years as if I were walking the streets of Jerusalem. I intimately understood Christ's pain on the cross and realized how empowered He was from God to be able to withstand temptations on earth and the pain of Calvary's cross. I realized how perfect He was as He overcame those temptations and the hours of agonizing forsakenness.

I understood that all humans sin and often give in to temptation. Yet I saw that Christ didn't give in to the same temptations. Because He is God, He is holy and blameless and therefore incapable of sinning. Only a perfect, unblemished sacrifice is worthy of holding the high title of Judge of the Universe and sitting at the right hand of the Father.

In front of the bookshelves were tables with toys and gadgets I had never seen. I moved towards one small device and picked it up. I could see it was a motor of some sort, but needed no fuel or electricity to run. Its wheels began to turn simply by my wishing for them to turn. (In heaven, we do not have to touch things to make them work. We wish for things to happen and they do. But, of course, our thoughts have to remain in harmony with heaven.)

I returned the toy to the top of the opaque table and moved into the next room. It also contained interesting items and gadgets. There was a huge box embedded in the wall above a shelf containing an extraordinarily complex computer-like device. Because of my interest in gadgets, and fearing I would not leave the room if I began to play with it, I didn't approach it.

Everything in this home was spiritual in nature. Nothing was corruptible nor could decay. Even the physical forms were manifestly spiritual: the fruit from the heavily laden trees outside, for example, contained no rot, bugs, or blight. Each tree created a different type of fruit that looked and tasted different. If the fruit was not eaten, it simply fell to the ground and immediately disappeared.

I began to see how poverty in heaven was impossible. No spirit being would be allowed to starve or suffer, as each of these delectable fruits was abundant and remained available to all. (Spiritual beings do not really need to eat any of the fruit; the fruit is simply a manifestation from God that all needs are immediately met in heaven.)

My thoughts moved me into the front yard. The view down the hill was breathtaking. I saw large homes dotting the hill for what seemed to be miles. Each home had its own garden and unique architecture. I saw many spirits of persons who had died; they would often visit these homes, as if in eager anticipation of their loved ones' arrival.

While standing there, my mind raced with the realization that one day I would return here—forever. The numbness was gone, the clarity was resounding. I knew that there were an infinite number of pleasures available here. There were no limits to the realm of heaven.

Everything was absolutely complete. Earthly fame and fortune meant nothing here. There was no fortune to be gained because great wealth surrounded me and could be enjoyed merely by recognizing it.

I also realized that those who had lived lives of darkness on earth and had barely made it here would be shocked to find such contrasts. In fact, many of those who had barely made it into heaven, perhaps whispering their need for forgiveness on their deathbeds, could scarcely accept all that God had prepared for them in this world. For many of them, it would take a long time just to learn how to accept the abundance available to them in heaven.

I understood the importance of learning kindness and giving on earth. When we struggle to do what is right and attempt to think right thoughts, even when the temptation to do wrong is so overwhelming, we grow spiritually. Learning to give and sacrifice on earth is immediately rewarded in heaven because heaven is a place of perfection.

*   *   *   *

I heard the voices of my family. I was back in my room. My spirit was elated. I felt at peace with myself. I had been drowning in depression, but now I felt well. As I remembered my life on earth, with all of its troubles, a pang of fear pierced my heart. But immediately I heard a voice say to me, "Don't be afraid. All is well with you."

I looked up and glanced outside my window. The true meaning of life enveloped me. Existence was wonderful! Sacrificing for the sake of others was worth it all. I knew I no longer would live my life in darkness but would walk in the newness of life.

Chapter 3

▼

TELLING OTHERS

Nearing the evening of the third day of my vision, I found myself wandering outside the house. My body was drained. I fell to the ground with my hands on my face, reflecting on the majesty of the last three days. I was overwhelmed by the sights, sounds and feelings of this heavenly ecstasy.

I recalled the three promises given me. The first promise was for healing—mental, physical, and financial. The second was of a dynamic and exuberant life. The third, and most profound, was that I would return to the heavenly world in my changed body and only then would I be able to experience the glory of the spiritual realm.

I wanted to continue to experience the feelings and pleasures that will be given only to those who choose to spend an eternity with God. But finally, late in the evening of that third day, which was a Sunday, I felt overwhelmed and tired. I looked towards Christ. He nodded and smiled lovingly in silent understanding. Knowing that I had reached the end, He turned and walked away from me. His spiritual presence never left me, but I was never to see Him again in His ethereal glory.

At that moment my faith was unshakable. I felt I could move mountains. Although I was not commanded to do this during the vision, months later I began writing down some of the things I had learned and been told, including every detail of emotions I had felt.

I felt obligated to tell others about my vision. I had just concluded the most incredible experience imaginable. I simply had to let the world know what had happened to me. I felt like shouting from a mountaintop to any one who would listen everything I had seen. Christ was real! God was real! Heaven was real!

*   *   *   *

The next few days I remained on a spiritual "high." After returning to college on Monday, I smiled at every one I met in the corridor. During class I was more attentive to the instructors. My comprehension became clearer. I felt energetic. That week I basked in the memory of my vision.

But gradually, my life returned to its pre-vision state. I had rejoined the unhappy, earthly world, and the experience of the vision became a distant memory. Daily, I struggled to convince myself that the vision really happened. The two worlds—the spiritual and the physical—remained chasms apart. This world seemed gloomy, dirty, and filled with anger and hostility; eternity, in contrast, was full of peace and harmony.

As the spring term of my sophomore year at the University of Portland concluded, my ecstasy from the vision was completely gone. I couldn't understand why after such an incredible experience God would allow these foreboding feelings to once more engulf me. I had assumed from the vision that everything would be different. I had been promised so much, and I wanted those promises to be fulfilled *now*. I longed to be back in the spiritual realm.

(Later, I was to realize that returning to the normal was good for me. It is not God's will for humans to live in a constant state of heavenly ecstasy on earth. Our mortal bodies are not designed for such; when the apostle Paul received a heavenly vision, it was so powerful that it blinded him. He had to wait for a miracle from God to heal him; see Acts 9:1–19.)

In June 1978, my sophomore year finished on a down note. My grades plummeted from an A to a B- average. My junior year continued with more unhappiness, and my grades dropped to a C average. Meaning melted into questioning and doubting, and my depression deepened.

At the time of the vision I had felt such power from God that I just knew something tremendous was about to happen in my life. In fact, although Christ had mentioned nothing about timing, I believed that what He had promised me was going to occur quickly. To me this meant weeks. Was I going to win the lottery? Was I to inherit some wealth from an unknown rich relative? I lived each day with the great expectation that something unusual was about to catapult me into wealth.

However, as week after week passed with no change, I realized that my thinking was flawed. God's promise to me was not necessarily immediate. I was devastated.

Then one rainy Sunday morning, I heard a message in church (the Damascus Church in Damascus, Oregon, which I had started attending when I went to college) that greatly affected me. "Preach God's message," the pastor said. "Christ's message to you contains a lot of power and meaning, and simply by releasing and sharing it with others you will blessed."

My ears perked up.

"Has God revealed something special to you lately? Then voice that experience with others."

As I left the church that afternoon, I was filled with a desire to talk about my vision with others. The pastor's message was loud and clear. I had to proclaim to others what I had learned from my vision. There is life after death! There is a heaven! There is hope!

My mood lifted. Telling others about my vision would make me feel better—and might remind God of what He had promised me, I reasoned. To my dismay, as I was to learn later, doing this was not exactly God's will for me at the time. Sharing my vision in 1978 was a bit ahead of its time. Modern-day visions and near-death experiences were not accepted by the general public until Raymond Moody's book, *Life after Life*, became a phenomenon shortly thereafter.

But I determined to do this, and my life went from the proverbial frying pan into the fire.

*   *   *   *

When I got home from church, the first person I saw was my mother, who was already home from the church she and Dad attend in Sunnyside. She was busy preparing dinner. I walked over to her.

"Mom," I said, "I would like to tell you about my vision I had recently." I began explaining to her about the house on the hill and the jubilance and joy that I felt there.

"In paradise," I spoke with authority, "there are none of the limitations that we experience here on earth." Elated that she was listening intently, I continued, "And God has chosen me to do great things in life."

She smiled at me, yet showed no enthusiasm. Fortunately, she did not ridicule or cajole me. In fact, she seemed to ponder the idea that something had actually happened to me. A few days later she quoted from Scripture: "It is true that God works in mysterious ways. As the Bible says: 'Young men will dream dreams and have visions'" (Joel 2:28).

With this tiny bit of belief from another person—even if it was my mother—I assumed I was on the right track in telling others about the vision. When I returned to school on Monday, I proceeded to tell a few of my closest friends about it. At first, each listened intently, as if I had great news for them. I related to them about the struggle up the hill and the mansion that was waiting for me at the top, and how everything related to life now.

But their expressions at some point always turned to disbelief. What I was telling them was just too bizarre for them to accept. I was naïve enough to believe that those I told would say, "Yeah! Great, Dan! I'm so happy for you. This is so great that God is going to heal you." Instead, the look on their faces said, "Yea, right! YOU got the vision that we've all been waiting for! *Good for you, Dan.*"

I wondered if this was what Joseph in the Old Testament went through when he told his parents the vision he had from God about the sun, moon, and eleven stars. His parents seem to take his vision at face value, but his brothers sold him into slavery. Fortunately, none of my friends sold me into slavery, but they did think I was nuts.

After a few days one student, who had in the beginning seemed to believe me, chided me. "Dan, hang in there and you'll get over this." He patted me on the head. "Each one of us, at one time or another, is given to fanciful imaginings. We all have too much to drink and then see visions of sugarplums dancing in our heads. If you wait long enough, these psychic divinations will go away."

His vain attempts at humor did not amuse me. I looked up, seeking immediate help from God. Yet He remained silent. I felt humiliated and alone.

The lukewarm response I received from family and friends puzzled me, yet I remained undaunted. I was determined to tell the world—even against the still, small voice nudging me to be silent about my vision at this time.

With continued rejection, however, I began to feel angry with God. I lamented, "Why didn't I die and go to heaven to stay rather than just get a glimpse of it in a vision?" The tension I felt between living with spiritual promise while enduring the pain of this world was at times overwhelming.

Yet I felt it was right to pursue the promise God had given me. So I decided to expand my audience—a wish that was granted one fateful Friday in late winter of my junior year.

*   *   *   *

The class was Religion 202: Judeo-Christian Culture. This was going to be my day. I would finally tell about my vision to a larger audience.

That day there were only about twelve students in class. The instructor, Sister Theresa Fisher, was a young, petite woman. Her small body, adorned with a black habit, was almost consumed by the classroom lectern as she stood behind it. Today, her topic was about faith, hope, and miracles.

At one point, one of the students raised her hand and asked, "Do you believe that the miracles as described in the Gospels actually occurred?"

"Yes. The miracles as described in the New Testament actually occurred."

The student accepted her response but continued, "Do miracles happen today?"

Sister Theresa looked across the room. "I believe they do. Does anyone have a story to relate about a modern-day miracle?"

I pushed myself up from my desk and stood next to my chair.

She pointed to me. "Yes, Dan, do you have something to say?" I hesitated, wondering if I was about to do the right thing. All eyes fell upon me. The class became silent waiting to hear my miracle.

"I would like to relate to you a vision that I had over a three-day period of time . . ."

I began to tell the class about the vision. I talked about the house on the hill. I described my great struggle up the hill. I spoke about the city of light and the platinum-colored lake.

At first, the students seemed spellbound. Then as I began sharing with them the promises that God had given me and were available to all, they began to stir restlessly. Realizing they were not receptive to spiritual matters, I began to feel uncomfortable. My message was falling on deaf ears.

One of the students began snickering. Another whispered, "I think he must have seen a UFO!" Still others placed their heads on their desks in vain attempts to hide their laughter. Before long, the entire class began to erupt.

Devastated, I quickly sat down. Sister Theresa tapped her pen against the lectern and called the class to order. She seemed somewhat embarrassed for me, but, like my mother, I think she believed me. She took the story at face value, was glad for me that God had promised me all those things, and left it at that.

But my classmates' reactions humiliated me. Fortunately, this class was the last one of the day. At the end of the hour I quickly ran out of the room and headed for my car. I couldn't escape my classmates quickly enough.

The following Monday, as I went from class to class, it seemed as if everyone was staring at me and thinking I was a kook. The next day, as I was heading to biology lab, I met two of the girls from the religion class. They stared at me for a minute, then one of them pointed her finger and began laughing. She whispered to her friend, "He claims there's a God and heaven! He's under the delusion God promised him some sort of supernatural success in life!"

Deeply hurt, I turned and quickly disappeared into the biology lab, taking my seat and hoping no one else would notice me.

On another day, Charlie, another student from the religion class, called out to me, "Hey dreamer! Any more visions today?" I felt like an outcast. Clearly, the students at this private religious school, none of whom knew me well, were just not interested in hearing about personal, spiritual matters.

One Friday in particular I dreaded going to the religion class. As the hour approached, I headed towards the room, but then stopped and paced for several minutes outside the door.

Having waited until I felt I could wait no more, I pushed the door open and stepped into the room, which was dark. A movie projector was running. I glanced towards the screen at the front of the room and saw that the movie *Jesus of Nazareth* was being shown. Right at that moment in the film, a beam of light shone down through a window and onto Mary's face. An angel spoke through the light. "You are the mother of God's Child."

Before I reached an empty desk, all eyes turned towards me. The class stared at me for several moments in disbelief. Though they later seemed to consider this incident just a coincidence, no one teased me again about what I had said.

All in all, I told about twenty people of my vision. And until this book, I never told another soul.

Chapter 4

▼

LIFE CHANGES AND
LESSONS LEARNED

That disastrous day in religion class was the worst of my life. My ego was crushed, my faith in God challenged, and my spirit bruised. What had God done to me? Why had He abandoned me yet again?

There was to be no rich uncle, no winning lottery ticket. And now, this humiliating experience. How was I to save face?

Yet even after this, I still believed that God would someday fulfill the promises He had given me in the vision. For now, I needed to figure out a way to get on with my life.

One of the results of telling others about my vision was that my depression lifted a bit. Whether the humiliation was greater than the pain from my depression, or that God began easing the depression—or both—I do not know.

I realized that I was going to have to accept life the way it was. God had given me the vision, and He was going to have to fulfill it His own way. I had to step away from my interpretation of the vision and allow Him to implement its true meaning—in His way, in His time.

So I began to change my focus. Slowly but steadily, I allowed the vision to take a back seat to other things. I began to rearrange my priorities. At that point, education became the most important thing, and I realized I needed to get serious about finishing my degree. I began hitting the books once more.

Since I really enjoyed working with computers in high school, I chose computer engineering as my program.

In the fall of 1979 I applied to and was accepted in the computer engineering program at Portland State University. Because it was a state school, PSU was far cheaper than was the University of Portland. It was also closer to home, and the change of venue provided some needed relief. I even was reunited with some of my old high school and junior high friends who were students there.

One of the first courses I took my senior year was in clinical psychology, which greatly interested me. I skipped ahead in the textbook several chapters and found a story about a woman who seemed to be as unhappy as I was. She had experienced very high "highs" offset by very low "lows." She would spend months in the doldrums. Yet she apparently had it all. She was married to an attractive, wealthy man who had provided her everything. She had three adorable children who loved her. She lived in a big house and drove a luxury car. Why wasn't she happy?

Her story fascinated me because I could relate. The book said she was diagnosed as a manic-depressive. I wondered if this was my problem as well.

Nothing I had tried up to this point seemed to permanently cure my depression. The textbook implied that only drugs and help from a psychiatrist could help cure a manic-depressive. But I wasn't so sure that I wanted to take lithium or visit a shrink.

My depression continued until midway through the first semester of my senior year in November 1979. About that time I finally began to feel God's presence again. So much of my depression had been caused by burnout from studying, having to work too hard, and constantly being in debt. Now that I was well into my last year of school, I began to see the light at the end of the tunnel.

Finally, at age twenty-one, I left school with a degree in hand and began searching for a job. In 1981, IBM had just introduced its personal computer in the marketplace, so I had found myself in the right place at the right time—confirming to me that ultimately, my choice of majors was made with divine intervention. Because both my degree and my work experience during my senior year were computer-related, I received several job offers in quick succession.

I accepted a well-paying position as a computer engineer for a company in Beaverton called Teneron. With my income, I bought a condo and a car, and within three years all of my many purchases were paid off, though I still had a few outstanding debts. Best of all, my depression had completely lifted during that time. By taking my focus off of problems and by concentrating on my work, I had finally found relief.

I relished the fact that my dependence upon my parents and the low-paying, part-time jobs I had throughout college were gone. One day I stood overlooking that same cliff where I had contemplated jumping off and killing myself a few years earlier. I lifted my hands into the air and shook my head with glee. I yelled to God.

"Finally!" I heaved a great sigh of relief.

God was beginning to fulfill His promises to me— slowly, but surely. I realized anew that He is *so* patient. Just like in my vision, over time the hill is traversed, the ladder is climbed, and life's meaning becomes clearer as we follow the path God lays out for us. The first promise fulfilled was that of an exuberant life. The realization of this gripped me. I no longer needed relief when I would experience a bad day. I would calm the panic, slow the pace, and breathe deeply. I would have faith and realize that better days were ahead; the problems would be solved.

My career blossomed and I was happy living on my own. By 1985 I had built a computer consulting business in which I could work only one or two days a week and still maintain an independent lifestyle. At the ripe old age of twenty-five, I was financially independent.

Even my love life had changed dramatically. I became involved in a loving relationship with a beautiful girl named Veronica. When I first met her in the singles' group at the Damascus Church in 1980, I was immediately drawn to her. At 19, she was a natural beauty, with long dark hair, deep brown eyes, and a shapely figure.

She was attracted to me as well. She liked the fact that I seemed to be more "in tune" with God than her last boyfriend.

Still feeling a bit shy and with lingering self-doubt, I worked up the nerve to ask Veronica out on a date. To my surprise, she said yes. So we went out for pizza in Sunnyside.

I fell in love with her. For a year we continued seeing each other and did things with the church group. Our relationship became very strong.

At Christmas I opened a thin, delicately wrapped package that she had given to me. It was an Amy Grant album, with a picture of the young singer on the cover. I stared at the cover and then looked into Veronica's face. "You look just like she does!" I smiled as I stared into her eyes. "I know," she replied as she moved her face to within inches of mine. "I asked you if you thought I looked like anyone famous. You said you thought you had seen someone like me but weren't quite sure who it was. I just decided to help you out a bit!"

After about a year of dating, Veronica wanted our relationship to become more permanent. She began dropping hints of marriage. She also wanted to take our physical relationship a bit further.

I had always felt that God's will must lead every aspect in my life. In fact, until I feel that it is the Lord's will for me to do something, I usually wait. I wasn't quite sure that He wanted me to marry Veronica. Besides, I felt I was too young and not yet ready at that time to make such a commitment.

I continued to date Veronica for two more years. I loved her but liked the relationship just the way it was. But that wasn't good enough for her. Finally, she said, "If you won't marry me, I'll find someone else who will." Veronica made good on her word. Shortly after, I drove by her house and saw a strange car parked in her driveway. I went to the door. "Alex" answered it. I was devastated.

The next day I called Veronica. She told me we were through and that she had been seeing Alex for several weeks. Clinging to God's love for me, I didn't lapse back into depression, though the sting from our breakup lingered for about a year.

*   *   *   *

A recession hit the Portland area in 1985, and my business declined a bit. I saw this as an opportunity to rest, so I took a few weeks off and visited the Oregon beaches and the mountains. Too much time off, however, made me restless. I decided I needed another life change, so in September I moved to Los Angeles, hoping that a change from rainy Portland to sunny L.A. would help me completely get over Veronica and that a new job would energize me.

After finding an apartment in the foothills of the Sierra Madre Mountains just east of L.A., I thought I had arrived in heaven. The weather was beautiful (seventy-five degrees and sunny the winter I moved there) and the lifestyle was laid-back. After one day of searching, I found a job working for a computer company close to where I lived. During my four years there, I bought and sold real estate, traveled in Europe and dated a few attractive women from Beverly Hills. I wondered if I had found the good life for good.

In addition to real estate, I also had invested in some bank certificates of deposit and computer stocks. During the late 1980s, interest rates were high and CDs performed well, as did high-tech stocks and bonds. I believed that both California and my own life were on a one-way track upwards. I felt I could do no wrong. But I was in for yet another rude awakening.

In October 1987, the second-biggest hit the stock market. Along with many others that day, I panicked because I had mistakenly felt that the stock market could not go down. So I sold the stocks I had. A day or two later, again mistakenly thinking that the stock market would continue downward, I converted the money from the stocks into gold. Both decisions were huge mistakes. The stock market quickly recovered from its "correction" and the gold market crashed. Fortunately, I held only a few percent of my total net worth in stocks (and later gold), but the losses still hurt—and taught me a valuable lesson. I fell prey to the temptation to overreact when the first sign of negative change appeared.

I learned my lesson well. Today I am still heavily invested in bonds, CDs, and real estate, but I react differently to downturns and other corrections in the marketplace. I see them as temporary situations that will eventually return to normal, and probably sooner than later—a financial lesson that applies to other areas of my life as well.

The Lesson of True Wealth

My California experience taught me several important lessons. The first was that wealth produces more stress and strain than it does happiness and fulfillment. At one time I owned several homes and expensive cars. Each of these, of course, required monthly payments, insurance, and upkeep. Yet none of the many worldly thrills that I experienced in my twenties can compare to my relationship with God.

God's ways do not fail us. No matter how much money I had or didn't have, God was always there for me. He looks at money in a neutral way—it's neither bad nor good. Money neither condemns us nor saves us; it's merely a modicum of purchase. And the more we use it to purchase things that benefit others, the more the money can make us happy—and the more freedom we can enjoy when we do have it.

Clearly, God was behind the success that I had achieved both in Portland and in Los Angeles, but the fact remains that His promises are unattached to worldly success. In fact, while my worldly success came about as part of the fulfillment of His promises to me in the vision, I also believe that to Him, our worldly success contains little meaning. After all, we take nothing physical with us when we die. The only things that contain meaning are those that are given back to Him and used for His glory.

All the combined wealth in the world cannot save one soul nor add even one day to our lives. The only things that count—the things that will last for an eternity—are giving and loving, learning and growing in our relationship with God. Although these are not seen as desirable or as badges of success here on earth—in fact, they are often seen as foolish and as missed opportunities—they are really the opposite. They are the substance of spiritual life and heaven, an eternal life that begins on earth. Acts of kindness and compassion done in this life will shine brightly in the spiritual realm and will be rewarded eternally.

True wealth on earth is not the accumulation of money and possessions but is the by-product of meeting other's needs. Rather than ask, "What can I do today to make more money?" we need to ask, "What can I do to meet other's needs?" Money should not be the goal; service should be.

The source of true happiness is the abiding presence of Christ. I call this "Living in the House of God." The Crystal City that I saw in my vision contained within it the glory of God. His spiritual essence emanated from the city—harmony, fulfillment, and justice. Everything we say and do is exposed in the light from that Crystal City. God hides nothing and allows us to hide nothing.

If we rely upon earthly wealth to make us happy, we will never find true happiness because there are too many surprises. About the time we think we are getting ahead, another expense comes due, the car breaks down, or the IRS declares our favorite tax loophole null and void and we are hit with interest and penalty payments.

God has to be involved with both failure and success for us to make sense of them. If we believe our success is not of God, we begin to attach ourselves to our success and worship it as if we are the sole owner of it. On the other hand, if we fail without God, then we believe that our failure becomes a permanent part of our lives and all is hopeless; we feel we will never get through the failure no matter how hard we try. I felt that way during my depression. I couldn't understand why it was lasting so long. It seemed that it would never go away.

The trouble with hopelessness is that it leads to a sense of desperation that causes many people to give up on life entirely. Satan tries to make us think that failure is permanent and that there is no solution. But failure is never permanent.

God is a miracle worker. In the midst of my depression, He wanted so desperately to heal me, but I had to ask for healing first. Part of the nature of God is the allowance of our free will. He guarantees none of us success or paradise, but He does guarantee us the chance to choose them. We must choose to live with God.

The Lesson of Renewal

The second lesson I learned in California concerned renewal. When we fail, God assures restoration afterwards. He gives us sufficient time to recover from the pain of failure. But we must remain careful during these times of tranquility. Overconfidence can set in, and if we're not careful we'll be back where we started.

The Christian life is all about enduring a short season of hardship for the sake of a future, eternal bliss. God showed this to me in the vision as I climbed up the hill toward the house. I did not build the foundation, or the walls, or the completed structure—God did that. My job was to climb the hill to get to the house.

The Lesson of Simplicity

The third lesson I learned, another one of God's immutable laws given to me in the vision, is that the best things in life are the simplest. It is far easier to maintain one small house and an economical automobile than it is to maintain three big houses and several luxury cars. It is far better to invent a device that is simple to use, easy to understand, and quickly reproducible than to spend years toiling on something that seems so complex as to have no end to its design flaws and is too difficult for the average consumer to comprehend.

An example of this is the personal computer. Years ago when computers first appeared on the scene, these massive, complex machines filled entire rooms. Only engineers with years of experience could understand and use them. Today, personal computers, some as small as the size of your hand, are easy to use. The smaller, simpler, and easier these machines become, the more people will use them.

We also must keep the day-to-day affairs of our lives uncomplicated. We must avoid becoming involved in too many activities or be too free with our "just between friends" conversation. We don't have the time to work three jobs, raise two kids, and worry about how we are going to tell our best friend that she simply doesn't know how to handle her man. Our lives are far too short to become this complex.

God's spiritual laws are immutable, and ignoring them comes with a price, as I discovered. The great film director Cecil B. DeMille once said, "We cannot break God's laws; we will merely break ourselves against His laws." I had to endure three horrendous years in order to find out who I was and see a tiny part of who God is and what eternity with Him will be like. So it is with every life. We must endure suffering for a season to enjoy the goodness available to us tomorrow.

Chapter 5

———————▼———————

SEVEN STEPS TO OVERCOMING DEPRESSION

Over the past twenty years, I have formulated (through experience) some basic ideas of what can be done to overcome depression at the onset. Many of these ideas are very simple but effective. They have come about through "minor" miracles as an answer to prayer from God. (In any attempt to overcome depression, I strongly believe that God has to be involved with the process.)

I have experimented with several different avenues of overcoming the depression I had during college. I eventually summarized the general elements into seven basic steps.

The vast majority of the technical material listed below has come from a book called The *Complete Handbook of Nutrition*, by Gary Null and Steve Null, originally published in 1972 and reprinted by Dell Paperbacks. Also, much of the information about bioflavinoids and Pycnogenols has come from Richard A. Passwater, Ph.D., who has done much research on how antioxidants affect the body.

Before reading this chapter, it is important to understand the intent of the information presented herein. I do not mean to suggest that following these guidelines will automatically cure your depression. There are no radical types of therapy presented here. I'm merely attempting to provide insight into how God helped me to overcome my depression and to suggest other tried-and-true methods that have helped others increase their overall health and sense of well-being. Above all, you must understand that depression is a very serious illness and may require the help of a medical profession as a first step in alleviating its effects.

Step 1 :
Recognize the signs of depression.

When I went through my depression, I hurt like heck. I would sit on the couch in my parent's living room and hold my head in my hands. I couldn't fathom what had caused me to feel so blue. During my vision I felt good all the time. Now, again, I felt intensely unhappy. Was this to be my permanent condition?

I tried several things to rid myself of the blues. I breathed deeply; I even panted to the point where I was about to pass out. I closed my textbooks and took long breaks from studying. I tried forcing myself to sleep late into the morning. All to no avail. I was still plagued with insomnia, heaviness of the heart, and feelings of hopelessness.

Day after day, I hopelessly tried to pinpoint the cause of my unhappiness. Did college make me feel depressed? Did my lack of social life make me unhappy? Was it restrictions placed on me by my parents?

It was all of these, and it was none of these. My depression could not be traced to any one specific source. It was a combination of many things: a chemical imbalance, poor environment, and the rude awakening I received in college to what had been a fairly sheltered existence.

The tornado of emotions continued swirling about in my mind.

Depression convinced me that life (and God) had been cruel to me. It robbed me of the joy I knew as a child. I wanted that happiness back! But how could I get it?

Gradually, I discovered I was not the only one struggling with depression. Jim (not his real name), a friend of my mother, was 76 years old. He and his wife loved to travel. They would average about four vacations a year and always spent a month or two in Hawaii enjoying the view of the ocean from a high-rise hotel deck. One day while mowing the front yard of his home, Jim grabbed his chest and dropped to his knees. Seeing him through the kitchen window, his wife quickly dialed 911.

Jim was rushed to the hospital. He had had a stroke. His recovery was slow and painful. For several months he was unable to do all of the things that he had done before. Severe depression set in. He could hardly move without struggling for every breath. He felt like giving up.

Another friend of the family, Ruth, is a 60-year-old retired teacher who had to have a mastectomy. She and her husband of 35 years had enjoyed a very active sex life. When the cancer was discovered in her breast, she endured a near mental breakdown. She thought her sex life (and hence, the rest of her life) might as well be over with.

She spent a great deal of time going from doctor to doctor hoping against hope that the diagnosis was incorrect. As it turned out, however, the first diagnosis was accurate. A radical mastectomy was the only solution. Her greatest fear had been realized. Before, during, and after the surgery, Ruth became a recluse. Permanent depression became her lot.

Signs of depression

One of the symptoms of depression is insomnia. Another physical symptom is feeling heaviness (pain) in the heart. This I had in droves. I would place my hand over my chest and stick my tongue out hoping to choke the pain out. I would sigh heavily and pant, trying to hyperventilate myself into unconsciousness.

Other symptoms include migraine headaches, an inability to concentrate, withdrawing socially, and chronic fatigue. When children are depressed, they can be impulsive and have tendencies towards acting out anger through violent means. They may have Attention Deficit Disorder (ADD). Symptoms for teenagers may include drug or alcohol abuse or affiliation with gangs.

Sources of depression

Depression stems from two basic origins—either internal or external sources. Internal causes stem from chemical or hormonal imbalances. For instance, serotonin may be lacking. This is often treated with Clomipramine. In women, depression is very often caused by an imbalance of hormones, usually estrogen. But levels of testosterone may be low as well. Estrogen or testosterone therapies, often given in the form of pills or injections, can solve these problems.

External sources of depression usually are created through a number of circumstances. Often, depression is caused by a loss of something—a marriage (through divorce or death), a home (through catastrophe), a job, or a child. These are devastating misfortunes. It may take years to overcome them. Rebuilding one's life after such a disaster can be a monumental task. Getting as much professional help as possible must be a priority.

My dark days of depression did not come about from a single source. Mine was due to both internal causes and external events. I had low levels of hormones, though when I was in school, a low level of testosterone was not confirmed to cause depression in men. As mentioned, I also endured the insecurity of being too deeply into debt and felt fatigue from working several jobs and carrying too many credit hours at school.

Step 2 :
Let others know you have
a problem.

During my three years of depression, I suffered in silence. Knowing what I now know, this is not what anyone should do. My chronic depression seemed as if I were crawling through a dark, suffocating tunnel from which I was unable to extricate myself. I could see no light and kept turning tight corners in my effort to escape; but I simply ended up returning to the same place. Sometimes you need someone to take you by the hand and lead you out of the darkness.

Ironically, my attempt to overcome depression on my own actually extended it. Today, I know I have many friends and family members who would have supported me had they known I was hurting.

Let your family know of your struggle. If none of your family members will listen, then find a friend or a spiritual leader. Share with them and talk out your feelings. Unfortunately, I was shy and cringed at the thought of sharing my innermost thoughts with my family. I thought they would see me as a kook and say something like, "We don't have these problems in our family." I simply thought they would not understand.

But sometimes we need to take risks. We need to talk, especially when we are hurting. If your friends or family try to give you solutions that you are not quite ready for,

you need to ask them to simply listen and try to understand your feelings.

Telling others that you are depressed can be hard to
do, but it is no reason for shame. You should not be
embarrassed. Most people you seek out will listen to you
and will attempt to help however they can. Your friends
and family are not as unapproachable about your pain as
you might think.

Step 3 : Determine to be an over- comer.

If we're not careful, depression can consume us to the
point where we are mentally, physically, and spiritually
debilitated. That's why another critical step in dealing
with depression is to determine that you *will* overcome.

Though I wanted to rid myself of my depression, I made
the mistake of withdrawing. I wanted to hide, be alone,
and not get involved in the real world. But I should have.
When circumstances seem at their worst, that is when you
must try hardest to rein in thoughts of hopelessness.

Everyone lives through times of great pain, whether
physical, emotional, spiritual, or a combination thereof.
Like David in Psalm 22, we feel as though God has abandoned us. During these times, we must understand that
God is working through our pain and eventually will restore
us to our days of happiness and joy. We must avoid at all

costs the luxury of self-pity. We must have faith that things will get better. We must determine to pull it together.

Recently, I sold a piece of property on contract. For two years, payments were made to me in a timely fashion. Then, suddenly, in July 1998 payments stopped. I was forced to file a lawsuit. Because of the value of the property, the person involved chose to litigate every step of the way. The temptation to feel self-pity became strong as I realized I had done nothing wrong. This is how self-pity creeps into our lives—through our knowledge that we have been unjustly wronged. Yet allowing self-pity to control our lives is deceptive justification. Satan likes to deceive us into thinking that we should be justified in feeling sorry for ourselves. I thought that the legal justice system would adjudicate in my favor in a timely manner, but this was not to be. The case continued in litigation for months.

Just like Joseph in the Old Testament, who was unjustly sold into slavery by his brothers, I felt betrayed. Yet because I did not allow myself to indulge in self-pity, I was able to keep a clear head. I prayed that God would provide me with a good attorney, and He did. Through my lawyer I was able to apply constant pressure on the person who had defaulted. By keeping self-pity under control, I was able to allow my lawyer to do his work professionally. (The case eventually was worked out equitably between the parties.)

Self-pity robs us of our most valuable asset—our ability to live life to the fullest. It stifles our dreams and deadens our senses. It creates inaction. It denies us the use of our normal thought processes. It can create panic attacks or make us physically sick. If we allow it to, self-pity can rule us.

Step 4 :
Identify and use your "trigger events."

Another important step in your plan to overcome depression is to write down your goals. Be specific. Rather than writing, "I want to be happier," or, "I want to lose weight this year," set more specific goals, such as, "I will jog three miles today," or, "I will stop eating cheesecake every Sunday."

Make your goals realistic. If you are just starting out on your road to recovery from depression, start with small steps. If jogging three miles seems to be too daunting or not eating ice cream every day seems to be too huge a sacrifice, then start with something easier. Jogging down the street or skipping the ice cream every other day might be a better way to start. Once you have succeeded with the small steps, you can more easily move on to the larger goals.

Depression is best overcome not by fighting it head-on but by changing directions. We become mired in depression by keeping the same mind-set and doing the same (wrong) things over and over again.

Joe says to himself, "I hate my job. I hate this career. But it's another dollar so I'll stay with it. My wife will kill me if I even threaten to quit." Problem is, Joe has been stuck with the same job for years.

Sally says to herself, "I'm too fat. I don't like my hair. I'm so disgusted with myself! I think I'll have another piece of chocolate cake." Problem is, Sally has been attempting to bury her sorrows in the refrigerator far too long.

To overcome bad habits that keep you mired in depression, think in terms of doing new things. Develop a new mind-set. There are numerous steps you can take to break old habits. For example, when I had a long way to go to complete my college degree, I stopped thinking about all of the things I did not have and concentrated on things I did have in the present and would have in my future.

My senior year became a turning point. The closer I got to graduating and putting the awful years of failure behind me, the more excited I got. I looked at graduation as a percentage. I said to myself (at the beginning of my senior year), *I have already passed through 75 percent of my college classes. The other 25 percent should not be so bad.*

I call these mind-changing (and life-altering) steps "trigger events." Many trigger events include exercise regimens or dietary changes, but they all have one thing in common—they interrupt our pain with positive input. Determining to use trigger events to change your life takes boldness and the will to act on them.

I have discovered riding a bicycle around my neighborhood gives me great pleasure and stifles the blues. My home is near the top of a hill, so I push myself hard to make it to the top without stopping. The hill is so steep and my exertion so great that physical exhaustion overwhelms any mental pain. Once there, I rest a bit and enjoy the beautiful view. This type of exercise is one of many successful trigger events for me.

I also belong to a health club. I would recommend joining a health club to anyone fighting and struggling with depression. Not only do you have access to a variety of weight machines and exercise equipment, but you also have access to trainers who can help you shed fat and build muscle. As a bonus, you can form friendships with other members of the club.

Getting in shape builds self-esteem. Even if it takes several months, determining to lose five pounds can be your important trigger event to take your mind off of your unhappiness. Trigger events change your focus from a self-absorbed, usually negative introspection to a positive external goal.

The following is a list of suggested trigger events that you can use to get your mind off of your unhappy situation and live life anew:

- Take up a new hobby.
- Sign up for a night class at your local community college to brush up on a lost skill, such as cooking or painting.
- Make a change at work—wear jeans on Tuesday instead of Friday.
- Take a different route to work.
- On a cold day, fix yourself a steaming cup of hot chocolate, sit down in a comfortable chair, and enjoy your beverage at a leisurely pace.
- Visit your favorite coffee shop and indulge in a wild mocha fantasy.
- Mix up a cup of your favorite herbal tea.
- Bake a batch of cookies.
- Buy a plane ticket to see your long-lost brother.

- Take a trip to the beach.
- Pick up the phone and call your mother.
- Hop in the car and visit a friend.
- Volunteer one evening a week to help out in a local soup kitchen.
- Work in the garden.
- Call your sister just to chat.
- Begin writing the novel you have always been fantasizing about.
- Watch your favorite movie.
- Write down in your journal what you would do if you had all the money in the world, then begin to do it even if you don't.
- Get the kids some cross-country skis and head to the mountain.
- Plan your next vacation. Pick some place exotic like Hawaii or Aruba.

To overcome fear or sleeplessness:

- Invite your nephew or niece to sleep over with you.
- Sleep with your teddy bear. (Yes, its OK for adults to have teddy bears too!)
- Read uplifting material such as Norman Vincent Peale's The Power of Positive Thinking.
- Make a mental list of all the blessings you've received in your life—all this is good

and worthy. (Hint: Begin with the letter A
and no doubt before your reach the letter Z
you will be sound asleep.)
●   Sleep with your Bible.

Once you get used to harnessing these trigger events,
you will become amazed at how creative you can be in
dealing with depression.

Step 5 :
Ingest healing foods, vitamins, minerals, and herbs.

Healing foods.

Advertisements for products that promise to help us
lose weight are everywhere: Jennie Craig, Weight
Watchers, Slim Fast. The diet industry is a multi-billion
dollar business. It promises great rewards—"A new you!"
Yet when they see models parade in front of their eyes
showing off their new bodies, many women are secretly
envious—and skeptical. *Are these models for real?* they
wonder. *Aren't they just made up for the camera?*

Oprah Winfrey has fought her weight loss battles along
with her viewers on television. Remember her jubilation
and the applause of the audience when she paraded in
front of them in size 10 jeans? Oprah was very honest con-

cerning her struggle with "the battle of the bulge." She confessed to trying many different diet programs, but none had worked. Why hadn't she found success? Because, like so many of us, she liked food—and lots of it. To lose weight, she finally came to the realization that there is no shortcut to victory and looked for a diet that best suited her. Over time, she learned that dieting can become a part of her daily routine. She began substituting baked for fried chicken, began to eat potatoes without sour cream or gravy, and made raw vegetables a daily snack.

Losing weight is a combination of exercise and proper diet. This is not to suggest that our exercise must be an uncomfortable regimen of pumping iron and running a marathon each week, but it is a daily process of change. We can still eat good tasting food; we must simply change what and how much we eat. Rather than indulging in a steady diet of red meat and sweets, we can change our primary staples to vegetables and legumes. (In the future, soy and bean sources will be made into products that taste very similar to the harmful ingredients we now use. Favorites such as meat, lobster and even fried foods will be replaced with substitutes that have similar tastes and textures as these, but little fat.)

Dieting can be fun and rewarding. We simply have to incorporate a few minor changes of habit. Mix up your menu a bit. For example, one day have brown rice and squash, and the next day have navy beans and strawberries. Dieting success is achieved more through making small daily changes rather than counting on drastic changes to lose weight all at once.

Exercise also can be fun and rewarding. Studies show that even a slight increase in exercise, especially in the elderly, has a profound effect on both quantity and quality of life during the golden years. As with dieting, mix up your routine. Rather than go to the gym to exercise, for instance, use the stairs three times instead of once to head to the laundry room. While cleaning the house, put on your favorite music and clean to the beat.

I do a lot of natural things to exercise—things that are also productive, such as planting flowerbeds and gardens, hand tilling, hand harvesting, mowing the lawn, raking leaves, and cutting and stacking firewood. Other enjoyable outdoor activities include biking, swimming, hiking and participating in sports such as soccer, baseball, basketball, football, volleyball, racquetball, or tennis.

Modern research has shown that even a slight reduction in calories can increase life span. For reasons unknown, when the body recognizes a reduction in calories, it more efficiently utilizes the calories it has. Fat begins to burn away, the muscles tone, and vitamins and minerals are more effectively incorporated into organs and tissues. The good news is that a slight reduction in calories is relatively easy to achieve. By replacing a diet of red meat and fatty fried foods with vegetables and legumes, calories and cholesterol will be replaced with protein and nutrients. Exercising a little more each day has the same effect— calories are consumed, fat is reduced, muscles are toned, and the body becomes a far more efficient machine that will not only live longer, but will allow the spirit inhabiting it to enjoy a far greater quality of life.

Another technique to use to reduce caloric intake is to slow down while eating. We are better off eating several small meals throughout the day than devouring a couple of large meals. The less we eat and the slower we eat, the more efficiently our bodies can metabolize the calories. The stomach begins processing food several minutes after the food passes the mouth, esophagus, and upper intestine. However, the stomach doesn't feel full, now matter how much we eat, until about 20 minutes after we swallow. If we take smaller bites and wait several seconds between each bite, our stomachs will feel fuller sooner, allowing us to eat less.

Much of the time, we eat simply for flavor and to fill an empty stomach. We eat quickly because we are afraid we will feel too full before we can get the last enjoyment out of all the goodies we place on our plates. This is a bad habit. But like any other bad habit, it can be broken. But it won't happen overnight. Bad habits are developed over the years. Slowly and surely, if we change our behavior one step at a time, we can overcome the temptation to overindulge.

To help you get started on modifying your food intake, I've included below a description of fats and other food types and how they affect our bodies.

Fats that are bad for you:

Saturated fat.

Saturated fat increases blood cholesterol. It is found in meat and dairy products and in coconut and palm oils. Specific sources include whole milk, cream, cheese, beef, lamb, pork, and ham. It is recommended that the daily intake of saturated fat be no more than 10 percent of your total diet. Those with high levels of cholesterol may need to reduce their intake of these products even more.

Trans fat.

Trans fat is found in oils that are hard at room temperature. Such oil is often used to make french fries, onion rings, crackers, and doughnuts. Many butter substitutes such as stick margarine or shortening also are trans fats. Trans fat increases LDL, or "bad" cholesterol, and thus is probably the worst artery-clogger available.

Fats that are better for you:

Monosaturated fat.

This type of fat is found in peanut, canola, and olive oils. It reduces levels of LDL (bad cholesterol) by slight amounts while not affecting the levels of HDL (good cholesterol). Be sure to read the labels carefully when purchasing cooking oils at the grocery store to get the highest amount of monosaturated fat possible.

Polyunsaturated fat.

Polyunsaturated fat is found in safflower, sunflower, corn, and soybean oils. Also, some fish oils are high in polyunsaturates. It reduces both LDL and HDL cholesterols. Your total daily intake from any fat should be no more than 15 to 20 percent of your daily calories.

Foods that help when you are feeling blue:

- Have your oatmeal for breakfast.

- Get a large salad bowl and fill it with dark lettuces, such as endive and romaine. Top it with pineapple. Use a low-fat dressing made from soybean oil (a "good fat") and vinegar.

- Smoked salmon or a large salmon steak grilled to perfection is both delicious and nutritious.

- Enjoy a whole grapefruit for breakfast, a mixed dish of vegetables for lunch, such as celery, radishes, beets, and sprouts, and a chicken chow mein dish for dinner. Keep vegetables on a tray in the fridge readily accessible all day. (It is better to eat a few light, healthy meals throughout the day than it is to have two or three heavy ones.)

- Drink vegetables in juice form. Carrots, celery, parsley, tomatoes, and even cabbage make great vitamin-filled snacks. For example, carrot juice mixed with cider made from crab apples is a tasty treat that provides large daily doses of vitamins A and C and aids with digestion. Fresh vegetable juice gives your body immediate benefit from the vitamins and minerals because they are not cooked out.

Foods to avoid:

- Refined sugar products: white sugar, commercial snacks and candies, most commercial breakfast cereals, cakes, pies, etc.

- Refined flour products: white flour, white bread, snack crackers, pizza crust, pastries, and pasta.

- Starchy foods such as baked potatoes loaded with butter or sour cream. When you do eat a baked potato, be sure to eat the skin.

- Processed foods such as frozen entrees or cellophane-wrapped packages loaded with preservatives. The more hand preparation the food requires, the better it is for you. Seek out whole foods, as close to their original form as possible.

If you have children, restrict their sugar intake. What children learn in youth they will retain into adulthood. Eating healthy is a good habit to start early on.

Healing vitamins.

Much study has been done on the power of antioxidants in enhancing the immune system, preventing cancer, supporting cell regeneration, and slowing the aging process. Recently, researchers discovered that antioxidants (largely vitamins A, C, B1, B2, B6, B12, and E) bind with "bad" free radicals in our bodies such as poisons and pollutants and render them harmless. Although it is wise to take no more than the recommended daily allowance (RDA) of each vitamin, we should take them daily.

Unfortunately, getting the right balance of these vitamins from the foods we eat is difficult. To help, you can take over-the-counter supplements that are labeled as a "complete antioxidant group."

The antioxidant group:

Antioxidants help protect the body from free radicals, which damage cells and reduce the effectiveness of the immune system, leading to susceptibility of viruses, colds and aging. Although antioxidants can be found in a diet rich in fruits and vegetables, our bodies are not able to obtain enough of them to combat our heavily polluted environment. The leading causes of increased free radicals include tobacco smoking, breathing polluted air, overexposure to sunlight and a poor diet. A high intake of antioxidants seems to improve the immune system, which in turn reduces the risk of infection, stroke and even cancer.

In addition, the body naturally generates its own antioxidant group: superoxide dismutase (SOD), methionine reductase, catalase and glutathione peroxidase. To boost this group, you can take additional antioxidants that are available as supplements: the vitamins A, C, and E, the mineral selenium and the hormone melatonin, among others. Each of these are explained in detail below:

[Many of these nutrients are recently discovered and are currently undergoing extensive research. Thus, recommended daily allowances are not yet established for many of the following food supplements.]

Vitamin A.
Helps maintain healthy skin, mucous membranes, bones, teeth, and vision. Found in fish and dairy products, it is stored primarily in the liver. Vitamin A deficient patients may be more susceptible to colds and flu as the cells lining throats and lungs have less stamina for fighting viral invasions. RDA: 3,000-5,000 IU (International Units, a basic units of measure for vitamins and minerals). Pregnant or nursing mothers should take 6,000 IU or more daily.

Vitamin C.
The most active nutrient in the body, Vitamin C helps fight colds and the flu. It was discovered in 1750 by Dr. James Lind. He noticed that British sailors on long voyages developed scurvy at much higher rates than those who sailed the coastline. He suspected it was the lack of fruits and vegetables in their diets. In 1795 the British Admiralty recognized Lind's discovery and began issuing limes as a shipboard staple. Until that time, more sailors died from scurvy than had been killed in all the maritime battles of history. RDA: 60 milligrams.

When I lived in L.A. I had a chronic scratchy cough. It is believed that breathing the smog-filled air there is like smoking half a pack of cigarettes each day. I had visited several physicians who almost always prescribed antibi-otics. Unfortunately, my body became immune to them.

One day, after praying about the issue, I ate breakfast at a restaurant. My meal included a large glass of orange juice. In the afternoon, I noticed that my lungs had a warm, itchy sensation, and I knew they were being healed. I racked my brain all day long attempting to remember what I had eaten that day. Then I remembered the orange juice, which is loaded with vitamin C. I quickly ran to the store, purchased a bottle of vitamin C tablets, and began taking the prescribed dose daily. Ever since, I have not suf-fered the normal winter coughs, colds, and flu.

Vitamin E.
Known as the "fertility vitamin," this may be a natural, mild aphrodisiac. Besides being one of the important antioxidant vitamins, it helps balance hormones in the body. If taken in recommended daily doses, it can slightly increase libido in both men and women. Vitamin E taken with estrogen works to stabilize sexual desire in menopausal women. Vitamin E also has helped me battle depression. RDA: 30 IU. *Note:* Women need to take at least double the RDA of this each day during pregnan-cy to avoid extreme mood swings due to hormone imbalances.

Selenium.
Selenium protects the heart, liver, lungs, and brain. It targets harmful hydrogen peroxide and converts it into water. One study has

found that men with the lowest levels of this antioxidant have a 70 percent increase in risk of heart disease. Selenium should be taken along with a complete vitamin supplement because its effect is enhanced with other antioxidants, primarily vitamin E.

Glutathione.
Glutathione is part of the body's waste disposal system. It inhibits cellular damage from free radicals. It combines with selenium to produce glutathione peroxidase. Scientists have found that people 60 and older with heart and joint discomfort problems have low levels of this nutrient.

Superoxide Dismutase.
Superoxide Dismutase affects the heart, lungs, central nervous system, and gastrointestinal tract by reducing free radicals. Cutting-edge research is being conducted to reveal how this powerful antioxidant effects the aging process. Dr. James Fleming of the Linus Pauling Institute of Science and Research inserted extra copies of the body's "ageless" (Methuselah) genes into experimental fruit fly embryos. Those that underwent this procedure were found to have increased levels of Superoxide Dismutase and ended up with extended life spans.

Melatonin.
One of the most powerful antioxidants, melatonin is an anti-aging hormone similar to the human growth hormone (HGH) and dehydroepiandrostone (DHEA). This hor-

mone may be the best free radical scavenger
available. Melatonin permeates every type of
cell in the body. It protects the cell nucleus,
the structure that contains DNA.

It is naturally produced by the pineal gland, a tiny structure in the brain. Produced in great abundance during youth, it helps create a smooth, youthful appearance and helps generate brain activity, especially concentration needed during learning. Reaching its highest level during puberty, the production of melatonin drops off steadily as we age.

Melatonin has been found to prevent cancer, heart disease, stroke, and hypertension. It also revitalizes the immune system and may have a major role in the production and balance of estrogen and testosterone, both of which may prevent and slow the rate of progress of cancers and diseases of the reproductive system.

Because natural melatonin production declines as we age, we can change our lifestyle to increase its effect. The level of this hormone increases with darkness, so we should avoid exercising late at night because exercise reduces the production of melatonin. Instead, exercise early in the morning (when production is at its lowest), outdoors and bathed in sunlight, if possible. Eating also affects the production of essential hormones such as melatonin. If our eating (or exercising) habits are out of rhythm, our hormone production will be too. Avoid stimulants such as coffee, tea, or soft drinks before bedtime. Eating and drinking stimulate digestive processes rather than melatonin production when hormone production should be at its highest. When taking melatonin as a supplement, be sure to ingest it in the evening, as its effects will work with the production of the natural hormone. If grogginess increases when waking up in the morning, reduce the level of the supplement until the tiredness decreases.

Many of these antioxidants work in synergy with other antioxidants, so it is best to obtain these nutrients as a group. Special multi-antioxidant or "super" antioxidant formulas can be found at most health food stores in pills or powders.

The Vitamin B complex:

Vitamin B (Biotin).
This vitamin is so potent that any living cell has no more than a trace of it. Lack of biotin can lead to skin diseases such as Leiner's disease (redness or swelling of skin) or eczema. If any of these diseases are present, they can be controlled by injecting 5 milligrams of this vitamin intravenously. Sufficient amounts of biotin can be obtained from daily consumption of unpolished rice, soybeans, sardines, liver, cauliflower, or brewer's yeast.

Vitamin B (Folic Acid).
Used as a major metabolic building block, this enhances the creation of red blood cells and aids RNA and DNA replication. Helps prevent anemia. RDA: 400 micrograms.

Vitamin B (Niacin).

Another vitamin needed to ease depression, it aids in the metabolism of amino acids. Without it, complete personality changes have been known to occur. RDA: 20 milligrams.

Vitamin B (Pantothetic Acid).
Essential in the metabolism of carbohydrates, fat, and protein. Works as an antihistamine and is related to the production of cortisone. Lack of this vitamin can add to hair loss, cracking of fingernails or toenails, and depression.

Vitamin B$_1$ (Thiamin).
Lack of this vitamin contributes to depression. When taken in recommended doses, it helps keep the brain functioning normally. RDA: 1.5 milligrams.

Vitamin B$_2$ (Riboflavin).
This keeps nails growing and hair shiny. But excessive use of alcohol destroys this vitamin. RDA: 1.7 milligrams.

Vitamin B$_6$ (Pyridoxine).
Discovered in 1939, this vitamin was shortly thereafter synthesized. It is essential in building amino acids. Insufficient levels of B$_6$ result in central nervous system disorders and irritability. Good sources of this vitamin include beans, wheat germ, peas, potatoes, cabbage, and bananas.

Vitamin B$_{12}$ (Cobalamin).
B$_{12}$ has many cellular functions, but it acts primarily as a coenzyme in the production of DNA. It also stimulates blood cell formation. Without it, anemia can result. Because the vitamin was fairly recently discovered (1948), the recommended daily allowance has not yet been established. You can generally find this vitamin in sufficient quantities in liver, kidney, fish, most meats, and kelp.

Vitamin D.
Found in eggs, fish, meat, and sunlight, this vitamin helps create strong bones and healthy skin. It is one of the primary ingredients in medicines that controls acne. RDA: 400 IU.

Vitamin F.
This aids in the lubrication of cells and helps prevent cholesterol deposits in the arteries. Vitamin F is also necessary for normal glandular activity. No RDA has been established.

Vitamin K.
Because this vitamin helps our bodies avoid hemorrhaging by aiding in blood clotting, it is often given in large doses to patients after surgery who have been given blood thinners before surgery. However, vitamin K should not be supplemental by itself. It is fat soluble and

therefore easily toxic. You won't find it in very many multivitamin supplements because it is dangerous. A healthy diet provides all of the vitamin K that you need. RDA: 25 micrograms.

Vitamin P (Bioflavinoids).
Bioflavinoids help strengthen capillaries and prevent edema. Vitamin P helps regulate capillary permeability (P stands for "permeability"). It also synergizes with antioxidants such as C to increase their effect. Lemons, limes, and oranges are full of bioflavinoids.

Pycnogenol.
This works both as a powerful antioxidant and improves the effectiveness of other antioxidants such as vitamins C and E. It also protects brain cells and may help improve memory and reduce senility.

Healing Minerals:

Calcium.
This mineral works with vitamins A, C, and D to aid in blood clotting and in the activation of enzymes. About 99% of calcium is found in bones and teeth. A lack of it may cause osteoporosis (brittle bones) and a reduction in height. Calcium is found in green vegetables and dairy products. Bone meal, which is available at most

health food stores, can be taken when severe calcium deficiencies are found.

Iron.

Iron is found in red blood cells and aids in the production of hemoglobin, which is necessary for processing oxygen in the bloodstream. It works with other elements such as calcium to regulate the body systems. Lack of iron may lead to anemia and poor memory. Green leafy vegetables, raisins, and egg yolks contain large quantities of iron.

Potassium.

This acts as a balancing mineral; it feeds the muscular system and normalizes heart beat. A deficiency may cause irregular heartbeat, irritability, or depression. Sources of potassium include bananas, mint, bell peppers, chicory, and figs.

Zinc.

This mineral is a component of insulin and improves vitamin utilization. Without it, diabetes may result. It also is a major component in respiration and is needed for the manufacture of testosterone. Lack of zinc may lead to fatigue and lower sexual interest in men. Sufficient quantities can be found in liver or over-the-counter mineral tablets.

Healing herbs:

Herbs that help us feel better and live healthier have been known for centuries. Many of these can be found in American folklore or ancient Eastern tradition.

Garlic.
Garlic helps lower LDL, or bad cholesterol, and acts as a natural antibiotic.

Ginseng.
Ginseng gives comfort for headaches and backaches that often accompany depression. It also can increase appetites such as hunger, thirst, and libido, creating a "trigger event."

Grape seed extract.
Proanthocyanidin (Pycnogenol) works both as a powerful antioxidant and improves the effectiveness of other antioxidants, such as vitamins C and E. May help improve memory, reduce senility, and control depression.

Peppermint or Spearmint.
Soothing to the stomach, this aids digestion if taken after a meal.

St. John's wort.
This acts as a natural mood-lifter for some people. It works quickly, usually within five minutes of taking the recommended daily dose of 200 milligrams. However, use this with caution if suffering from depres-

sion; some people have a paradoxical response and become highly irritable.

Sassafras (and other green teas).
Often used to create tasty teas, this herb helps heal the body by cleansing it. Some teas contain small amounts of caffeine, creating a mild high.

Additional recommended food supplements:

Food supplements are important because the typical modern diet remains incomplete. We eat foods that are fatty and lack fiber, essential vitamins and minerals, and necessary antioxidants. Rather than encouraging us to consume that which is better for us, wealthy societies tend to accelerate our rate of disease because of our excess. Foods that claim to be "new and improved" or promise to taste better have become our staple diet. In reality, these expensive processed foods are loaded with the worst types of fat, sugar, and preservatives.

Ironically, societies with far fewer resources eat more nutritiously than we do. In the third world, diets consist of natural whole grains, legumes and beans, mostly brown rice with husk, fish oils, and soybean products. (The closer we can get to God's natural creation, the better off we are!) In addition, poorer societies are generally unable to afford adding the most basic of processed ingredients. These more natural foods afford less-developed societies the opportunity for healthier living, at least from a dietary standpoint. (The politics of some of these nations remains a whole different story!)

In North America and Europe, however, food supplements have become a necessity. I have detailed some of the more common supplements, their sources, and effects below: (Information taken from James and Phyllis Balch, *A-Z Guide to Supplements*, Avery Publishing, ©1998, pp. 127–148.)

Alfalfa.
Surprisingly, this leguminous plant is available primarily in liquid form. Alfalfa contains all known vitamins plus calcium, magnesium, potassium, and phosphorous. The minerals are in balanced form and synergize well with the vitamins. Alfalfa aids in the healing of ulcers, gastritis, asthma, high blood pressure, bleeding gums, infections, burns, and cancer.

Bee pollen and other bee byproducts.
Bee pollen contains the entire B complex, vitamin C, essential amino and fatty acids, enzymes, carotene, and a balanced mineral complement. It comes in a powdered form and should be consumed in as fresh a form as possible. If it is clumped or clings together, its effect is greatly reduced. Bee pollen helps fight fatigue, cancer, colon disorders, and depression.

Royal jelly.
Royal jelly is a milky substance that is a combination of both honey and pollen. It

has slightly higher concentrations of essential minerals, enzymes, and vitamins than
bee pollen. It is the only known natural
source of acetylcholine.

Brewer's (nutritional) yeast.

*Brewer's yeast is rich in several different
nutrient groups, including fourteen minerals,
most of the B vitamins, and sixteen essential
amino acids. More than half (52%) of brewer's yeast is protein by weight. Yeast aids those
with sugar imbalances, such as hypoglycemia
and diabetes, by improving sugar metabolism.
It is also good for eczema, heart disorders,
gout, and anxiety. Be sure to purchase nutri-
tional yeast, as baker's yeast robs the body of
essential nutrients and should be avoided.*

Fiber.

*Fiber is essential in reducing gastrointestinal
and colon difficulties. It also helps prevent
hemorrhoids, colon cancer, and sugar imbalances, such as hypoglycemia and diabetes.
Sources of fiber include whole grains (rye and
oats), brown rice, dried prunes, flaxseed,
beans, peas, and fresh vegetables. At least one
of these sources should be consumed daily.*

Kelp.

*can be purchased in granulated, powdered,
or tablet form. This seaweed is a rich source of
vitamins as well as many minerals and trace
elements. It is beneficial to the brain and its
tissues. Because of its iodine content, kelp has
been used to treat thyroid problems, and it
can aid in preventing hair loss and ulcers.*

Lecithin.
Largely composed of the B vitamin choline, linoleic acid, and linistol, lecithin is a lipid needed in every cell of the human body. Cell membranes and the sheath surrounding the brain are largely composed of lecithin. Lecithin is known to promote energy, increase brain function, and help repair liver damage due to alcoholism or poor diet. The elderly in particular should consume it because it controls high serum cholesterol and triglycerides. Recently, it was discovered that lecithin extracted from egg yolks may aid those suffering with chronic fatigue syndrome, herpes, AIDS, chlamydia, and rapid aging due to stress.

Mushrooms (shiitake and reishi).
Pronounced "shee-it-talk-ee" and "ree-she," these mushrooms have been popular in the Far East for more than 2,000 years. They strengthen the immune system by increasing T cell function. Mushrooms contain an assortment of amino acids, the B vitamin complex and vitamin D. The benefits of these mushrooms have been touted for generations by Asians to promote youthfulness and vitality.

Shark cartilage.
For centuries the Chinese have believed shark cartilage to be an aphrodisiac. It is also believed to reduce the effect of cancer by shrinking cancerous tumors. Recent research has shown that this cartilage reduces net-

works of blood vessels surrounding tumors and other places where blood vessels should not be, such as in the back of the eye (aiding macular degeneration) or in the lower thigh and leg (varicose veins).

AIDS, leukemia, and cancer can be treated in part by using a combination of the above remedies. The trick is to ingest slightly higher doses than the RDAs and do it consistently. If I had AIDS, the first thing I would do (after seeing a good doctor) is load up on antioxidants, pycnogenols, and fruit juices. I would exercise daily, dump all bad habits (such as smoking and excessive drinking), and train my mind to think positively all the time. For example, I would envision my antioxidants acting as the "power pills," as in the Pac-Man arcade game.

Overcoming depression through natural means requires a change of regimen—in fact, a change in *lifestyle*. Consistency is the key. If you take a few of these natural remedies once in awhile, they will not do you much good.

Step 6 :
Seek professional help.

You've probably seen the bumper sticker that reads, "Insanity is inherited—you get it from your kids." But depression is also inherited—kids can get it from their parents, grandparents, aunts or uncles. I have a great-grandfather who suffered severe depression; in the end, he took his own life. As my mother's family contemplated his fate, they realized that professional help and the medication available during his life possibly could have saved him.

In my own prison of depression, I did not seek professional help. Only through the miracle of God's intervention was I ultimately healed.

Clinical depression can be treated using a multifaceted approach, including various therapies such as counseling and drugs. Drugs used are usually grouped into six major classes—antidepressants, mood stabilizers, anti-anxiety agents, side-effect controls, psychostimulants, and hypnotics. The following drugs are the most widely prescribed for each of these categories:

Type
    Example   Drug
    Antidepressants   Prozac

This works to increase the availability of the brain's supply of chemical signals. The class of drugs known as tricyclic antidepressants, or MOA inhibitors, interacts with almost every other known chemical substance, including over-the-counter medications and most herbs. Be aware if you are prescribed a drug in this class; they can be of great benefit but must be used with caution.

    Mood Stabilizers   Lithium

Lithium helps regulate the central nervous system to moderate extreme emotion.

    Anti-anxiety Agents   Valium

Valium is used to control anxiety, seizures, or alcohol withdrawal. It slows down action in the brain and spinal cord.

Side-effect Controls (beta-blockers)
Inderal

Inderal controls high blood pressure, irregular heartbeats, pheochromacytoma, myocardial infaretion, anxiety, and migraine headaches. Its primary side effect is extreme fatigue and somnolence (or catitonia). A catatonic state is not desirable for someone already suffering depression.

Psychostimulants   Dexedrine

Dcxedrine increases mental alertness and decreases fatigue. In addition, it helps control behavioral problems, such as attention deficit disorder in children.

Hypnotics   Halcion

Halcion helps relieve insomnia by sending signals through the brain and spinal cord to create restfulness. It also causes the body to skip the REM portion of the sleep cycle. Long-term use of this medication is not recommended.

Seek professional medical help if depression persists or becomes so severe that you feel that you would be better off dead than alive. The bottom line to solving depression is to reach for as many sources as you can for help. Never give up. Scream and yell if you have to. Keep persisting until you find the right person or therapy that will help you.

Step 7 :
Pursue your dreams.

So much of depression is created by a loss of direction. As we become adults, we seem to lose our vision. We temper our dreams with the seemingly bleak or harsh realities of adult life. We need to be constantly reminded of the potential life we had when we were young. We need to renew our dreams.

This can be illustrated with marriage. When couples start dating, the relationship itself creates fantasy and giddy feelings. Somehow, several months after the marriage vows, that feeling of romantic excitement can die. Couples become entrenched in the routine of careers, deciding who cleans up the kitchen and garage on the weekend, and working feverishly just to get along. The honeymoon fades.

Granted, it is difficult to keep a marriage relationship at the honeymoon stage. It is just as difficult to continue pursuing our youthful dreams, but we must. The way we do this is by remembering events from our past, listing our goals, and determining that we will achieve them.

The first step is to write down your wildest fantasy. You need to think like a child. It could be anything from finishing college to finding a new career to taking an African safari. Then take that first step towards your goal. Place your list where you can easily see it every day. Eventually, you will gain enthusiasm and determination as each step toward fulfilling that goal is marked off.

Children rarely temper their enthusiasm. They want to play a lot. As adults, we need to play a lot too.

Years ago I posted on my refrigerator a list of goals that I thought were a bit fantastical because at the time I had no money. But I wrote them down and posted them anyway. The exact list was this:

- Buy a nice car and condo.
- Find a good job close to where I live.
- Find a pretty girl to date.
- Get over this horrendous depression!

All of these goals seemed impossible, yet because I had posted them on the fridge, I was reminded of them daily. Within one year of graduation, I had achieved all of these goals. I only wish that I had written these down while I was still in college in the midst of my depression. I am sure writing down positive goals would have taken my mind off much of my misery. Even the effort of writing down goals allows us to exchange negative, harmful thoughts with positive and constructive ones. It gets us dreaming and moving again!

Depression is like a dark spot on our ceiling. When we see the spot, we become obsessed with it. We see nothing but the spot. It bugs us. We think it is dirty. The spot makes our house imperfect and we worry that others might be staring at our spot too. It makes us unaware of all that is going on around us.

We need to change our focus. We need to place our hands on either side of our head and force our head downward, back to the reality of what's going on around us. And if we can't move our head for ourselves, we need to find someone who can do it for us.

We can envision changing our focus like this as "event redirecting." When we practice this, it helps us begin to control our situation and refocus our thoughts to what is really important.

Remember Jim, the fellow I mentioned earlier in this chapter? To begin overcoming his depression, he had to redirect his energy away from his disability and toward his ability. Jim began working with a physical therapist. Over time she helped him overcome his limitations. She began to show him how to move his arms and exercise his joints. Within a few short years, he was able to return with his wife to his favorite condo in Hawaii.

Ruth, the woman who had a mastectomy, began seeing a therapist. She was fitted with a prosthetic breast. Before long, she was able to accept herself as a sexually attractive person. The relationship between her and her husband returned to the love and compassion that had been its foundation.

Johnny, a friend of mine, lay hovering near death after a severe car accident. He had a broken spine and was told by the doctors that he would be a quadriplegic if he survived. Johnny did not want to go on. Day after day he prayed for God to take his life. Finally, one evening the dark clouds of death filled his room. He felt as if he were sliding into a coma as the darkness enveloped him. Suddenly, a radiant light burst through. Johnny recognized God in the light. Yet rather than usher him through the light as Johnny had hoped, God gave him a choice. A barrier appeared in front of him. "If you cross over this fence you will be in eternal rest forever. But if you decide to turn back, you will be commissioned to complete your mission on earth."

Johnny turned and looked back at the broken, lifeless body lying in the hospital bed. He did not want to return. He knew returning would mean pain, agony, and perhaps years of struggle through rehabilitation. Yet he knew that God had something great for him if he returned to his body. He almost felt compelled, as if he would be missing out on something beautiful if he did not. As if by command, he returned to his body. Although he endured months of painful rehabilitation, Johnny ultimately was glad that he returned to his body and this world. He is still restricted to a wheelchair, but he has successfully overcome his physical limitation and realizes that his mind is still intact and functions normally as it had before.

I remember a similar incident during my vision. While I was climbing the steep hill, Christ was standing at the top cheering me on. Exhausted, I felt like giving up. But He waved me forward. With His encouragement, I felt like I was an athlete whose team was trailing with only seconds to go in the game. I knew to succeed I must go on. The mystery of what waited for me at the pinnacle seemed too wonderful for me to quit right at the critical moment. Making the decision to continue took enormous strength and energy—more than I ever dreamed I had. But today I am so glad that I did. My three years of intense emotional pain and depression have transformed into more than twenty years of happiness and joy.

It is important that you remember that life's struggles are worth it. Through God, your pain and depression ultimately have a meaning far greater than you can ever imagine. Through persistence, will, and determination, your dreams may eventually become the reality that you have for so long hoped for.

Chapter 6

▼

SEVEN KEYS TO ETERNAL SUCCESS

One day as I came home from work, I walked up to my front door to unlock it. I reached deep into my pocket, but to my surprise I did not find the house key. I quickly turned around and headed back to my car. Inside the car I began frantically searching for the keys. In an instant, I found my key ring buried between the two front seats. I breathed a sigh of relief.

One of God's purposes for my vision was to teach me how to unlock the doors to the fundamentals of life. I began to analyze the different phases in my vision. Early on I had written down the outline of what I was taught. Now, I have boiled it down to seven keys. These keys illustrate the opening of the doors to our spiritual success here on earth as well to our future in eternity.

Key 1 : Self-worth

Of the three promises that God gave me during the vision, the first two dealt with my life on earth. God is not removed from the human condition. He is concerned with our earthly welfare.

One day, when I was eight or nine, two of my friends and I thought we would have a little fun and experiment with some matches and grass in the vacant lot at the end of the street. My father was watching me from our garage, and as I was halfway down the street he called out to me, "Dan, where are you and your friends going?" I replied, "We're going down to the vacant lot and do some experimenting." To say the least, my father was very curious about what the experiment was all about. I wasn't quite sure what we were going to do with the matches either, but my father quickly ushered me home and encouraged me to be more selective in my experiments.

God is just as concerned about our endeavors here on earth. He wants to direct our paths, and He will give us the confidence and abilities to do whatever He asks of us.

When I was a junior in high school, I had the honor of being FFA president. I remember the doubts I had about being able to perform the responsibilities of holding office. I had to stand up in front of large groups and conduct meetings every week. I faltered at times and even thought of quitting once or twice. My parents encouraged me, however, and I dutifully accomplished the tasks at hand. In the end, I felt very confident; I had completed what I had set out to do and had done it well.

Maslow, a psychologist specializing in human growth and development, categorized self-esteem under his "self-actualization" terminology. A healthy self-esteem is one of the most important factors in reaching our goals.

The first promise that was given to me in my vision was that of mental healing. In my vision, Christ used these words to me: *dynamic* and *exuberant*. *Dynamic* means to be vibrant, vigorous, compelling. *Exuberant* means to be fruitful and filled with life and abundance. I understood those words to magnify the hope of joy, happiness, and meaning. God was telling me to love myself in a positive way.

I often watch *Monday Night Football*. I can't help but be enthused by the cheering that goes on among the fans. The cheerleaders jump and shout and encourage fan participation. They are dynamic in their motions and yell with exuberance. This was what Christ said to me in the vision about how I was to live my life. I was to be dynamic in my daily life, pushing forward to reach my goals, and I was to be exuberant in my thoughts and words.

As I began writing down my thoughts after the vision, I glanced out my den window. I saw dark clouds covering the sky, but I knew behind the dark, ominous clouds the sun was shining. Dark clouds often represent the hardships and circumstances that surround our lives, creating in us depression, unhappiness, and despair. My mother and I were flying in a private plane from Portland, Oregon, to Vernal, Utah. As we took off and soared into the beautiful blue sky, we shortly came upon a wall of heavy, black thunderclouds. Becoming concerned, my mother asked the pilot, who was a personal friend of ours, how we were going to deal with the clouds. He replied with assurance, "We will rise above them." Within minutes we were riding high above the storm.

Through the climb up the hill in my vision, God revealed to me that in spite of the struggles, hardships, and difficulties we face, we must keep our eyes focused upward in order to soar above the snares of life that attempt to rob us of our joy and exuberance. We must believe in ourselves. We must carry on and pursue our dreams.

Key 2: Dynamic Purpose

Another promise God made to me in the vision concerned my life purpose. God's objective is for each of us to find our mission.

At the time of my vision, I was in a mode of indecision about what career I should pursue. When I first entered the University of Portland, my major was medicine. As the weeks progressed, however, I found myself becoming more and more discontented. During one of my premed classes, the professor went into great detail about the many specialties that are available in the medical profession. Somehow, I just couldn't get excited about any of them. Early in my sophomore year, I went on rounds with a resident physician at the University of Oregon Health Sciences Center. As we entered the rooms of various patients, he projected a spirit of negativism induced by overwork. At the end of the rounds I questioned him about why he had entered medicine. He mumbled, "Before you make the choice to become a physician, you'd

better make sure that is precisely what you want to do."
Even though he did it in a negative way, that man showed
me one life's important truths: we must be decisive when
we reach the many crossroads along life's pathway.

After thinking long and hard over the next few months,
I decided that medicine was simply not my forte. I realized
I was trying to pursue something that I was not emotionally equipped for. I could not handle caring for patients
who hovered between life and death, knowing that I
might make a mistake.

God often gives us answers based upon our own dis-
coveries as we put our interests to the test. Eventually, I
changed majors to computer engineering, and I've never
regretted that choice.

We need to learn to overcome indecision, which
often leads to a loss of purpose. Sales is a great profession that demonstrates this. I have a very close friend,
Jim, who is in multilevel marketing. I have observed
him on several occasions when he is talking to someone
on the phone about products he is selling. Rather than
be defeated by each objection the caller voices, he
responds with an upbeat question, such as, "Wouldn't
you like to save money, Mr. Jones?" or, "Can't you see
how this product would add quality to your life?" Jim
has learned to view obstacles simply as stairs to climb in
order to reach the top.

The second promise given to me also included financial
healing, which God gave. Even as a child, my dream was
to be financially independent. When I picked strawberries, my goal was to save my earnings in my piggy bank. I
always wanted it full. When school began I would get my
piggy bank and shake out all the coins and dollar bills and

go on a shopping trip with my mother. One summer I earned enough to buy a brand-new blue Schwinn bicycle.

The late Mother Teresa, a nun who worked among the poorest of the poor in Calcutta, India, knew that her purpose in life was to encourage and uplift the world's hopeless. Even when she was awarded the Nobel Peace prize, she was not deterred from her purpose to help the poor. She used the large financial reward to further her work.

God knows our inner being and that we all want to aspire to great heights. Financial prosperity is just one part of the many possibilities here on earth.

Key 3: Exuberant Faith

The weeks following my vision the glow of the experience began to fade. My emotions rode a roller coaster of doubt. I realized I would have to switch gears and determine to have faith that what I had experienced was reality. Questions constantly clouded my mind, but I was determined to exercise the expectations that I had been given in the vision. I began to sort out all of the negatives that filled my mind and replace them with the words that were spoken to me: "Exercise faith, Dan." I had to discipline myself to take this admonition at face value and expect the best.

Later on, I began to exercise faith when I began purchasing real estate. When I was twenty-one, I was offered the opportunity to buy my now-deceased grandmother's condominium. It was a step of faith. I had doubts about being a property owner. I took a great deal of time mulling the idea over in my mind before I finally made the plunge. I'm glad I did, because I still own the condominium today as a rental and it is worth far more than what I paid for it. The purchase of this property (along with others) has served a twofold purpose: it has provided families with a nice place to live, and it has proved to be part of God's second promise to me as a fulfillment of financial independence.

Another incident of faith occurred when I made a bold decision to leave Portland and move to California. In Portland, I had a good job that paid well. I loved the work and was treated well. However, I needed a change. I had written some thoughts on paper concerning my vision, including a movie version of the manuscript, and knew that I needed to move to Los Angeles to pursue this dream.

For several weeks I agonized over the decision. My family is very close-knit. I had four small nephews and two beautiful nieces, and leaving them would be tough for me. Yet, ultimately, I knew I needed this adventure. I could not live with myself knowing I had not given my dreams a chance.

When I finally decided to move, I broke the news to my family. They were happy for me and wished me well. Then came the good-byes. I loaded my Trans Am and headed for California. It took firm determination to carry through with my plans.

Arriving in Hollywood, I was dazzled. I figured this is where more of my dreams would pan out. But after many appointments with movie production companies and an equal number of polite rejections, I decided I had to enroll in a script-writing class. The benefit from this was that I met and saw some very important people in the film industry.

In the meantime, I had set up my residence in the beautiful town of Arcadia, nestled in the hills of the San
Fernando Valley. I found a job that was very rewarding
both mentally and financially. I ultimately came to the
conclusion that Hollywood was not the magical name it
appeared to be at first, but the four-year journey I spent in
California was blessed with serendipities all along the way.

This past Easter Sunday I noticed that a local television
station would once again broadcast the great epic *The Ten
Commandments*. The film portrays the journey of Moses
as he leads the people of Israel on an exercise of faith.
Moses was to lead a nation out of bondage into freedom.
It appeared as if it would be an insurmountable task.
Moses had just spent forty years in the wilderness. Now,
he was called to leave the quietness of the desert and con-
front Pharaoh.

The time had come for the reality of the promises to
begin. In spite of his doubts, he marched forward. Moses
had been given promises from God to accomplish this
task. God performed many miracles to help him move his
people into the land "flowing with milk and honey."

It has been more than twenty years since I had the
vision, but I know the vision was to tell me that our life
on earth is much like the life of Moses. We are wandering
for forty (or more) years. But God is with us along the
way. During our journey we are to always remember this
and keep our eyes focused upward.

God is a God of abundant life. He has given us years on
this earth to learn about Him and grow in our relationship
with Him, and we must use these years wisely. To fully
realize this, like Moses, we must exercise our faith.

Key 4: Work to Completion

Two of the most powerful principles we can follow are those of completion and perfection. Our life on this earth can be thought of as a mission as we do God's work to completion, yet we must let God perform the work of perfection. It is so important that we do not confuse the two. A major source of my depression came from the desire to be perfect.

As I attended classes at the University of Portland, I wanted to ace each test I took. This was my concept of perfection. During junior high and high school, I achieved A's easily. I became spoiled. But during college this was not the case. A's did not come quite so easily. I quickly learned that I would have to work very hard to achieve high grades. At times, I would receive a lower grade even though I had spent hours of intense study.

After college, however, I came to understand that what was important was the completion of the task—in this case, the test or the course—not so much the grade I earned. These challenges were a part of God working through adversity in my life to improve my character. I often had to maintain a "stiff upper lip" when my test scores were not to my liking.

Completing tasks is our job. Perfection of our work is God's. While attending college, I witnessed students dropping out of school. Conversing with one student who was quitting the engineering field, I asked, "Why are you leaving?" He replied, "The course is too hard!" I could relate, as I also took courses with such scary names as "Quantum Mechanics" and "Calculus with Static / Dynamic Applications."

I often think of how his statement has mirrored the temptation in my own life. The thought of giving up when difficult circumstances arise is overwhelming. We are tempted to divorce when our spouse is not treating us the way we would like, or we want to drop out of school when the teacher criticizes us for a poorly written paper. Yet perseverance pays off. For several decades now, I have been rewarded for completing a difficult college education. I have been given job offers that either require a four-year degree in computer engineering or pay more to those who have the degree.

When difficulties arise and we don't feel like continuing on, we must fight the feeling to withdraw. Every important project or task to be completed will be fraught with difficulty, setbacks, and the need for hard (and sometimes unrewarded) effort.

The temptation to quit often becomes strongest just before we are nearing the end. This is where we must fight the temptation the most. In fact, the closer we get to the end, the harder we must work and the more determined we need to be.

We often see the failure to exercise this principle in professional sports. Just at the point where one team is ahead of the other and the clock is winding down, the winning team gets a little too relaxed and too careless. This creates a great opportunity for the losing team to catch up and win a game that the better team should have won and could have won had they stuck to their game plan and completed their task.

We must not let partial success breed contempt. For example, an athlete who enjoys a multimillion-dollar contract may feel that both the money and the contract guarantee him success, no matter how bad his behavior may be. He may participate in drunken brawls or threaten the life of his coach, yet feel that he is immune from criticism or penalty. We must never give up the responsibility we have been given to use our skills to the fullest.

While struggling up the hill in my vision, the closer I came to the top, the faster and harder I needed to push. In fact, the closer I came to the top, the more enthusiastic I needed to become in order to get there.

Completion applies to accomplishing certain tasks in this world. Whether completing an education, planting a crop, or fulfilling a contract, we must work to complete something of value. Perfection takes completion one step further: it makes the struggle of completing the task meaningful. This is God's work. Completion is doable in human terms; perfection is possible only from God.

We often get caught up in expecting too much from ourselves or the people around us. Too often we concentrate on a missing piece. As we adults raise our teenage children, we remember how hard we worked as teenagers (or so it seemed) and become frustrated when they do not seem to work as hard. We concentrate on their small flaws rather than focusing on the overall positives that they bring to our lives. For example, seventeen-year-old Suzie may not keep her room as clean as we would like, but she enjoys picking up her younger brother from school every night and baby-sits him until Mom gets home.

This is like putting an entire puzzle together only to find that the final piece is missing. We look under the couch, remove everything from the closet, and frantically search high and low, afraid to run the vacuum. Our entire focus has been turned toward that missing piece. We must not do this. We must refocus on the entire puzzle and envision the overall picture. We forget that 99 percent of our accomplishment lay in putting together what is there. We must stop, pull back, and not fret that final piece. Once we do this, the missing piece will mysteriously reappear when we least expect it.

Completion is a process; perfection is the endgame. Completion is arriving at the top of the hill and walking through the unfinished house. Perfection is when Christ, as He did later in my vision, puts up the walls. Completion is finishing high school or college; perfection is God working in us to help us develop wisdom as we use our new knowledge.

Our task of completion on earth is never achieved. Once one project is completed, we must move on to another challenge and begin yet again. This is the cycle of our life on earth.

Key 5: Seek to Understand Hidden Value

There was once a builder who worked for a very rich man. One day the rich man asked the builder to construct him a beautiful palace. "Spare no expense," the rich man said. "I want this home to be made of the finest materials and have the strongest foundation. I would like it to remain for years as a legacy for the owner's children."

Immediately, the rich man gave his builder a great deal of gold to begin the project. The builder traded the precious metal and began building. Over the weeks, money continued rolling in. At first, the builder bought the finest materials, from concrete to lumber. He purchased the finest brick, mortar, and tile to embellish the palace.

Yet over the months, the builder became entrenched in his own problems. His personal bills began piling up and the project seemed to be taking twice as long as he had planned for. He could hardly wait to finish the project so he could be paid. He was concerned that the rich man would become impatient and would dock his pay if it were not done quickly and within the promised time frame.

At the same time, the resentment the builder felt toward the rich man began to overwhelm him. He felt jealous that he was working many hours of overtime to benefit the rich man rather than himself. The builder's wife complained constantly that he was spending too much time on the project and not enough time with her.

To speed up the building process, the man replaced his highly skilled and methodical workers with lower-skilled workers who "got the job done quickly." To hide much of the shoddy work, he erected fancy facades that looked good but could not withstand harsh weather. He began paying his personal bills with cash that he had saved by hiring cheaper labor and lower-quality materials.

Finally, the house was built. Upon hearing the news, the rich man quickly returned and admired the work. "It looks even better than the last home you built for me. How did you do it?"

The builder simply smiled and handed the rich man an
envelope containing a demand for his final payment.
"Please, sir. I am in dire financial straits. I have worked
long and hard on this home for you and my own home is
far behind in its mortgage payments. If you could pay this
today, I would be greatly indebted to you and will be on
my way."

The rich man waved the letter away and handed the
builder his own. The builder quickly ripped open the
envelope. He gasped in astonishment. He found his own
name at the bottom of the deed to the palace.

"For years you have been a good and faithful servant,"
the rich man beamed. "You have built many fine homes
for me and my family." He grabbed the builder's hand and
shook it vigorously. "Now it is my turn to reward you."

The builder turned away sadly. Needless to say, the
house did not make it through the first winter. It was not
long before the foundation cracked and the roof leaked.
Finally, the house collapsed into a great heap.

In my vision, I realized there were no shortcuts I could
take as I was climbing the hill. It didn't matter if I went to
the left or to the right or back down the hill again; ultimately, I needed to move forward and upward, many
times retracing the same steps I had taken earlier.

Waiting for me at the top of the hill was a beautiful
palace built by God Himself. No corners were cut; no
facades were used to cover up shoddy work. The house was
perfect in every way. I simply had to determine to move
up the hill towards the home. Although the direction I
traveled may have changed, God's pathway did not.

God does not shortcut the law of hidden value. The
greatest things remain unseen. It is not the things of this

physical world that we can enjoy for an eternity. It is only what we have given away from this world that will return to us. And the knowledge we obtain in this world, particularly through our pain and suffering, will enable us to have unique wisdom for eternity.

The following story illustrates this law of hidden value as applied in my childhood. As a kid, I was often egocentric and spoiled, and these flaws made me a bit blind to both the unseen (and often unexpected) serendipities that are available to us from God.

One of the things I did as a child during summer breaks was to work in strawberry fields. One particular warm day when I was about nine, my friend Carl and I were assigned to opposite ends of a row stretching from the top of a hill to the bottom in a large field. I had always prided myself on how fast and efficiently I could pick berries and how much money I could make in a short period of time. After noticing how small and sparse the berries were, I began to think that I was not going to be producing a lot that day—and thus not making much money. Nevertheless, I felt I could outperform Carl without working too hard even as I ate almost as many berries as I placed in the crate.

After about two hours of work, I had filled only one crate. As I passed Carl on the way to the cash table at the bottom of the hill, I glanced into his crate. It seemed to be only about half full. As slow as I was that day, I felt I was on my normal schedule of outperforming him anyway. As well, I noticed that he had moved only about four feet from his end of the row. "Better get cracking," I told him as I turned and walked away. "I'll be doubling you all day long if you don't step on it!" He smiled as I turned and placed the crate on the cashier's table.

After another couple of hours, I headed to the cash counter with my second less-than-full crate, then by noon, my third. After cashing in that last crate before lunch, I headed back toward Carl. I noticed that he had moved only about fifteen feet from his end of the row. I yanked the three one-dollar bills from my pocket and waved them at him. "See. Not too bad. The pickin's are pretty slim, but I'll bet I'm still doubling you! In fact, I'll bet you a root beer."

He smiled, stacked one full crate on top of one other, and pointed to two more. "Take those in for me will you?"

I stared at the crates for a moment, and then looked at him. "What's going on? These aren't yours, are they?" "Yes, they are," he smiled smugly. "And it looks like I'm going to enjoy that root beer!"

I stared at him in disbelief. "How'd you do that?"

"Look at this," he said as he placed the crates on the ground and then reached down and pushed some strawberry shoots aside. I stared at the bushes and gasped. "Those berries are huge!" "Yes, and there are tons of them!" he chided as he pushed more leaves out of the way. He looked around. "Can you believe how great the berries are here? I've been in seventh heaven all morning!" He picked up the two crates and placed them into my waiting arms. "You can join me at this end of the row after lunch if you want."

Of course, after lunch I joined him at his end of the row.

I had spent the whole morning working at the top of the hill where the berries were the sparsest while he was down in "berry heaven" earning more money without having to fret and fume over poor pickings. (Today, I realize that the flat area at the bottom of the hill was where the water and fertilizer had concentrated after running off the top of the hill, thus producing the abundance of luscious strawberries.)

How often we do not see the big picture! We become so focused that we see only what is around us, what is in our immediate environment. All we see is work, work, and more work. We work so hard to achieve a type of success that will not gain us much. I've never heard anyone proclaim on his death bed, "I sure wish I'd put in more hours at the office."

God offers a better way. We often think we have to be "good enough" to achieve salvation. God says that none of that is necessary. Success is merely giving, happiness is simply loving, and salvation is attained only through believing (John 3:16). Being forgiven is realized in our willingness to forgive others.

Our greatest successes are achieved through stopping in our tracks, looking around, paying attention to what God is saying to us, and then accepting the opportunity that lies on the horizon. Sometimes this requires changing direction, and that is done through making positive choices.

I did not have to build the spiritual house in my vision; God did that for me. My job was merely to climb the hill and get to the house. God provides a myriad of resources on earth for us—food, water, building materials, and even precious metals such as gold and sliver. It is not through our own efforts that trees grow. It is not through our own efforts that we reap a harvest. God created plants that produce seeds to replant and acres of earth to plant them in. We must never stop relishing and praising the creative power of God's miracle workings!

Key 6: Loving and Giving

Another thing I learned from my vision is that one of the ways to overcome depression is loving and giving to others.

The woman who won it all!

One day while surfing the TV, I stopped to watch an interview of a middle-aged woman who had just won a million dollars in the Powerball lottery. I watched as the reporters questioned her. "Are you going to buy a big home? Are you going to buy a Mercedes Benz? Take a trip around the world? Go to Disneyland?" The reporters eagerly awaited her response. She answered without emotion. "I have been volunteering regularly with charity organizations in Portland. Most of the money will go to the poor. I am currently satisfied with my house and clunker!"

The reporters stared in amazement as if she had lost her sanity. Most of us would have been jumping up and down at the prospect of upgrading our houses and cars and giving our jobs (and cantankerous bosses) the old heave-ho.

(Incidentally, most lottery winners never achieve the happiness that they had hoped the winnings would provide them and many end up in bankruptcy!)

Yet this woman had discovered a powerful secret to happiness on earth: amassing great wealth and clinging to it as if it were our salvation leads to emptiness. True happiness and joy come by giving a portion of our success to others. Although we live in a material world, we must keep

material possessions in perspective. The greater our own-
ership on this earth, the greater the responsibility we have
to share it.

Superman!

Actor Christopher Reeve fell from a horse and broke his
neck a few years ago. Ironically, the one who portrayed
Superman on screen is now confined to a wheelchair. He
needs a respirator to breathe for him. Yet his inner strength
is more and more evident. His mission in life is now one
of giving and loving and encouraging thousands of people
who have been hurt through similar tragedies. This is a
good reminder that tragedy does not separate us from the
love of God but can be another step up the hill towards
the mansion that awaits us in heaven.

Giving and loving in marriage

My mother and father have been married more than
forty years. I have taken notice of the giving and loving in
their relationship. Daily, they use the keys of giving and
loving to keep their marriage intact and to keep the family unit as one.

Applying the keys of giving and loving in a marriage
takes tremendous effort. It requires submission of our personal wills and desire for control, but the sacrifice is well
worth it.

Wanted child

When we use the keys of loving and giving, we build strong character. I heard about a man who is only thirty-eight years old but who lives in a nursing home. As a baby, he was diagnosed with spina bifida. Upon hearing this news from the doctor, his parents became resigned to the fact that they were emotionally and financially unable to deal with the situation. So they decided to give up the child for adoption. They knew of a single woman in their neighborhood who had been praying for a baby to adopt for years. The parents approached this woman. "Would you accept our child even though he is deformed?"

The woman gleefully accepted.

Through the years, the woman raised the boy as if he were her own. The new mother and adopted son traveled extensively—to Disneyland, the Eiffel Tower in Paris, and Times Square in New York. She cared for him for more than thirty years until her death.

My mother recently visited this man in the nursing home. He is always smiling, happy, and content. He does not remember any of his early childhood, but his positive countenance is a result of the attitude of this dear woman, who sacrificed a large portion of her own life to make better the life of an unwanted child.

Unhappy childhood overcome!

On November 18, 1998, about two hours into her program, radio talk show host Dr. Laura Schlessinger entertained a caller who complained that her foster child was doing poorly in school. The teenager had been in the new foster home for only a few months. The caller asked how strict she should be with the discipline because of the girl's poor performance. Dr. Laura immediately responded with some hard facts about the difficulties of being a foster child. The caller should love the teenager, invest time with her, and not discipline her for poor grades.

To illustrate how important love is to a child, one of my coworkers wrote a heartfelt letter to Dr. Laura concerning the pain of being abandoned as a child. Dr. Laura read it on the air. It follows here:

"I'm writing in regards to the woman who was upset because her foster child was doing so poorly in school. Your answer to her was so full of wisdom and compassion that it moved me to tears. That woman could have been talking about me. By the time I was fifteen, I, too, had been through several foster homes, some of them as damaging as my original family.

"One of my sets of foster parents was obsessed with my grades and behavior. They expected a very wounded, depressed, lost little girl to perform at a level equal to children who had been raised sanely and safely. They had me tested and discovered that I was bright and assumed that my failure to bring home straight A's meant that I was just lazy. Consequently, my inability to do well only enraged them, and after a year they finally sent me packing. This only further confirmed my belief that I was completely unlovable and made me crawl deeper and deeper into my shell.

"I believe that the caller was well meaning and
truly wanted to help this girl. She just needs to
understand that the poor child is probably so
damaged that all she can do for survival is to dis-
engage from her surroundings. What she needs
most is love, patience, and assurance that she is a
worthwhile human being and should not be con-
tinually handed off to a new set of 'parents'. I
suggest that the mother pull that little fifteen-
year-old girl into her arms and hold her tight and
tell her again and again how much she loves her
and how wonderful she is and that she is not
going to let her go. Trust me, that girl will
respond. Discipline is helpful, but love is what
will pull that child through."

Today my coworker is happy, healthy, and has found
her way in spite of a dark childhood.

Key 7: Believe in Eternity

Our choice for eternity is made on earth. One morning
when I was living in California, as I got out of bed God
gave me a vision of three doors looming in front of me
shrouded in a gray mist. (This vision, I believe, was an
answer to a prayer for wisdom in knowing how to explain
what eternal salvation is like to a skeptical engineering col-
league of mine.) The doors were of the same height and
width. I stared at them, wondering what they could mean.

My curiosity was aroused and I leaned forward to take a closer look. My eyes began to focus on a caption above each of the doors. Displayed on the door to the right was a picture of an eagle with outspread wings and a caption overhead that read, "All who pass through will enter paradise."

My eyes moved to the door to the left. A picture of a vulture was painted in black with the caption above that read, "All who pass through will forever live in darkness and will feel great pain."

The door in the middle had a brazen picture of an ostrich with its head buried in the sand. The caption above this picture read, "All who pass through will feel nothing."

I scratched my chin and squinted as I contemplated the three birds.

I stared at the vulture. It seemed to be glaring at me. It seemed to say, "Come on, I'm the easiest to open. Choose your own path! You can follow every whim that comes to your mind. You can enter into the dark side of life—crime, violence, drugs. Be free. God is not going to judge you! As long as you can outrun the law you'll be fine."

The bird with its head in the sand was interesting, almost funny. It seemed to be saying that it was all right to be thoughtless, to disregard the plight of the world, and to ignore God. I didn't have to be concerned with my future nor with eternity.

My eyes focused on the last door. This door only beckoned quietly. I knew that choosing the door of the eagle, the path of sacrifice, would take a great amount of courage, effort, and determination. "It's too simple," I said to myself as I tried to figure out which door to open. "It must be a trick!"

But God does not intend to deceive us. He is very clear. The logical choice is the way that promises eternal life. We must choose the door with the eagle on it, to follow the path of God. However, the temptation to open the wrong door and walk the wrong path is often powerful. Drugs, alcohol, and the many other temptations of life beckon us to open that wrong door.

During my journey through the dark tunnel of depression, I questioned the existence of God. I, too, fought with these doors.

Learning to choose the door of the eagle takes a deliberate act of faith.

Ironically, it takes the same amount of energy to believe that there is a God as it does to believe there is not one. The energy expended to open the door promising eternal bliss is the same as either of the other two. (I now understand that the distance traveled to the door of death was the same distance as to the door of life).

Hitler decided one of his goals was to conquer the world. His concept was based on the idea that he was greater than God. He had created the most potent military machine the world had seen. Ultimately, his faulty moral foundation led him to complete and utter failure. He had not taken into account that actions always bring consequences. In his attempt to conquer the world, he also tried to destroy an entire race of people. In the end, he became so despondent as the Allied troops stormed across Germany and into Berlin that he chose to commit suicide.

Within Hitler's bunker, you can envision the battle between God and Satan. Satan stands before God and petitions him concerning Hitler's early ending. "Lord, I would like to take this person to my realm. His choices in life were pleasing to me and not to you." God remains silent and allows Satan a few moments to expound the details of Hitler's life as Satan saw it. Satan states his case. God motions for the keeper of the Books of Life to bring them to Him. He opens one book after another, searching for Hitler's name, but to no avail. Finally, the books are closed. "You are right, Satan. This man must belong to you. His name is not written anywhere in these books!" And with that, Hitler's destiny is given into Satan's hands to do with as he wishes.

We must choose the door of the eagle. We must choose to rise above the discouragement and depression. The eagle is a door of freedom and strength of character soaring above the hardships of earth.

Heaven is all around us on earth too. We merely have to see it and believe it.

Heaven is looking into face of your child when she hands you a dandelion and says, "Mommy, I picked this just for you." Heaven visits us when we reach out to those in need or offer a word of advice to help. Heaven is stopping to smell the roses; it is time slowed down. Heaven is a moment of triumph when struggling so long to overcome a terrible tragedy.

Heaven is remembering the excitement of the first few dates with the spouse you have been watching television with for the last several years. It is sitting next to the one you love and snuggling. It can be planning a wedding, planning an anniversary, or planning for a first baby.

We will leave our greatest legacy not through our strengths but through our weaknesses. The greatest Man who ever lived died on a cross 2,000 years ago. A seeming failure, His death left a legacy that is growing stronger to this day. Against the backdrop of human depravity, spirituality is growing day by day. Christ's spirit of compassion has built many nations whose goal is to reach out to oppressed foreigners and has helped to destroy the walls of totalitarianism. We must not mock Christ but accept Him. Rather than disbelieve God, revere Him.

Believe you can change the world, but start in your neighborhood. The little things count—the smiles displayed, the gifts given. Avoid the cacaphony of negative political opinion. Keep the tools in your toolbox unlocked and available. Be ready to accomplish your tasks alone, but be willing to work with the team when the need arises. Trust those around you. Create new ideas and new ways of attacking your own or other's problems. New ideas are not necessarily bad ones; they may stimulate an entirely new and successful direction. If all else fails, be willing to work harder. Make a contribution every day.

Chapter 7

▼

PERSONAL MIRACLES

So much that has happened in my life, in addition to the vision, has been miraculous. In this chapter I share with you some of the miracles from my life as well as the lives of my friends and family. After reading these stories, I hope you agree with me that God truly works in mysterious ways.

God's reasons for performing miracles are not always known, but one truth remains: He is a miracle worker by nature. From the moment of our birth until we draw our last breath, miracles occur throughout our lives. Even the beating of our hearts is a reminder of God's miraculous nature.

Water into Wine

I relate this story from the Bible because it shows that the Christ of my vision is extremely attentive to even the smallest detail of our lives. We must firmly believe that when we ask for bread, He will not give us a stone (Matthew 7:9).

Jesus and His disciples had been invited to a wedding feast in Cana of Galilee. In the Jewish culture of the New Testament era, weddings were a great time of rejoicing and celebrating—the parties could last for days. The best food was prepared, brought forth, and displayed on elegantly decorated tables. No expense would be spared for such a glorious occasion. Jesus and His disciples were mingling among the crowd, enjoying the festivities of the wedding, when suddenly a cry was heard above the fun and laughter—"No wine!"

Jesus' mother, who was standing nearby, immediately approached Him with this seeming dilemma. "We have no wine!"

Jesus saw the concern in her face and sensed the frustration in her voice. He said to the servants, "See those six stone water pots sitting over by the wall? Go fill them with water."

The stone water pots were very large, holding between ten and fifteen gallons each. The servants began carrying the heavy pots out to the city well. Pot after pot was lowered into the well and then laboriously pulled up by rope, each overflowing. As quickly as the men could, they returned each pot to where Christ was standing.

"Now dip your ladle," Christ said to a servant after the last pot had been brought, "and take it to the master of the feast." The servant quickly obeyed. "Here," he said as he handed the ladle to the headwaiter, "try this." The master of the feast took the handle and raised the ladle to his lips. He stared in disbelief. "This is wonderful!" he exclaimed as he returned the ladle to the servant. "Why has the best wine been saved for the last?"

They had never tasted such exquisite wine.

A Supernatural Healing

A young girl of sixteen lay in an unconscious state in a hospital, hovering between life and death. A deadly disease was surging through her body, robbing it of its lifeblood. A group of people was hovering over her, praying that God would heal her and restore her health.

Not long before, a young medical doctor had arrived from a large hospital in New York City and settled in the small town of Pendleton, Oregon. This doctor was called in on the case. After examining the patient, he pointed out to his colleagues the unusual marks on the young girl's body. They all stood baffled. The young doctor related how he had just witnessed a case where he had seen similar markings on a patient in the New York hospital. He diagnosed the disease as Rocky Mountain spotted fever. It was caused by an infected tick, he said, and he knew of a twelve-year-old boy who had died from the disease.

Over time, the patient began to get better. The prayers continued. However, there remained a question as to whether her gangrenous limbs could be saved. Amputation seemed of the essence, and so it was decided to remove her left foot and ankle.

Finally, after weeks of prayer, her body was healed of the gangrene as well as the Rocky Mountain spotted fever.

A miracle? I believe so. Even with the loss of part of a limb, *my mother's* life was spared during a time when so many had died from a disease for which there was no cure.

A Miraculous Sign

Wes Shultz (not his real name) was one of my best friends in school. He was always kidding me that I was "too religious" and no one needed that "God stuff" in life. In spite of the teasing, we had formed a close kinship. After school he and I would play tennis and often program the school computer.

I was an avid reader, while Wes found reading a bore. He had better things to do. One day I was browsing the shelves of a bookstore. One particular title caught my eye. It was called *Beyond and Back*, by Ralph Wilkerson. This book contained stories of people who had very deep faith in God and had heavenly near-death experiences. I bought the book and took it home.

I became so intrigued after reading the book that I read it again. The pages soon become dog-eared, and over time a crease formed right down the center of the cover from top to bottom. After finishing the book again one evening near the end of my freshman year, a strong urge came over me to give it to Wes. I slapped the book shut and set it down on my dresser.

It sat on my dresser for several weeks. One morning I realized it was near the end of the school year and I hadn't yet given the book to Wes. I grabbed it and took it to school. At the end of the school day, I encountered Wes in the breezeway.

I called out to him, "Wes, I have something for you!" As he approached me, I handed the book to him.

"What's this, Dan? You know I don't like to read," he joked as he took the book.

"I have a strong urge to give this book to you, Wes. I feel there is something in it for you."

He looked at the cover skeptically. "How odd," he mumbled to himself. He managed a halfhearted smile as he glanced towards me skeptically.

"*Beyond and Back*? I hope this is an adventure story." Reluctantly, he placed the book into his backpack.

As Wes was turning to leave, I reminded him, "Be sure to read it." He turned back and responded, "I'll give it a shot, Dan, just for you!" He turned and headed towards the line of buses waiting to take us home. Months later, while readying some tractors for the fall hay harvest, I got the news. Wes, my best friend, had drowned in a boating accident. My heart sank. I immediately thought of the book that I had given him. Had he read it? Had the message been clear to him that there is a God and life after death? Now I understood why God had urged me to give him the book. But the question remained—had he read it?

I sent up a silent prayer to God. "Please give me a sign that he received the message You had for him in the book." After three days of intense mourning, I felt peace in my spirit.

Later on, as Christmas approached, I was visiting with Jim, another friend of mine who had not known Wes. As we were talking, Jim said, "Dan, I have a book I want you to read." He walked over to a desk, picked up the book, and handed it to me. I noticed the title: *Beyond and Back.* "Where did you get this book?" I asked.

He replied, "A friend of mine gave it to me and I feel you should read it too."

I stared at the book. I immediately noticed the crease on the cover. It looked just like the book I had given to Wes! As I grasped the book firmly in my hands, I looked up into the sky and smiled.

"Hello, Wes," I said. "Someday I will see you again …"

I am not sure whether the book given to me was the exact one I had given to Wes, since Jim had never met him. But, miraculously, it was the same title and did have a similar crease on the cover from the top to bottom. I took these two events at face value and never felt agony about Wesley's death again.

A Glimpse of Eternity

In 1978 my grandmother was diagnosed with pancreatic cancer. I visited her as she lay in her bed at Good Samaritan Hospital in Portland, surrounded by family members. I cringed as I noticed they were squabbling with one another. I couldn't believe they could be so cantankerous around their mother's deathbed.

I looked at my grandmother, who seemed to be smiling in spite of the commotion around her. "You kids don't need to fight—it's so beautiful here!"

How could my grandmother, whose body was racked with pain, find so much comfort and joy? I believe this can be explained in only one way: God had given her a miraculous glimpse of the eternal, heavenly home that lay shortly before her.

That evening she died.

My Journey to School

I was a trumpet player in my grade school band. One evening a month during the school year we would hold a band concert in our school gym. Our band instructor was very prompt. He insisted that we arrive half an hour before the concert to warm up our instruments. If a student was late, the band instructor would glare at him, frown, and call out his name, demanding the student come in after school one day to practice. It was very embarrassing to be tardy!

On the evening of one concert, my mother said, "Dan, I can't take you right now to the school, but in twenty minutes I can." I became very upset with her. I dreaded being reprimanded in front of the whole class if I were late. I hurriedly grabbed my horn and, putting my jacket on, said, "Mom, I'll see you at the school. I'm going down to Glen's. I know they will be leaving soon, so I'll catch a ride with them." Then I ran out the door.

Glen's house was just a few blocks from mine, so it didn't take me long to jog there. As I knocked on the door, I noticed the garage door was shut. I knocked again. No answer. Just as I turned around I saw their car turning the corner. I stood wide-eyed in his driveway. I looked at my watch—it was getting late. I spun around looking toward my home, but I figured my family had left by now.

The school was four miles away. I would never make it on time. Tears began to well up in my eyes. I didn't know if I should go home or start to walk. I wish I hadn't been so impatient! I could just hear the band instructor yelling at me. Taking a deep breath, I decided I would head for school anyway, figuring that maybe I could get there for part of the concert.

Within a block of Glen's house, a dilapidated Plymouth with tail fins pulled up beside me. A gray-haired man rolled down his window.

"Young man," he asked, "are you on the way to school?" For a minute I hesitated, knowing my mother had always warned me against riding with strangers. I again looked at my watch; the concert was about to begin.

I looked at the elderly gentleman. His eyes seemed to have a twinkle in them. He looked very kind. "Yes, I am." Before I knew it, he reached over and unlatched the car door. "Get in," he said, "or you will be late." So I got in.

He was wearing a threadbare khaki overcoat, and his hair was a bit tousled. I was just about to ask him who he was when we pulled up in front of the school. I jumped out, eager to get to the band room, hoping the band hadn't left for the auditorium. But then I realized I had not thanked the man for the ride. I turned around to thank him, but no one—no car, nothing—was in sight. When I entered the band room, the band was just lining up to go out on the stage. I was right on time.

The Guardian Angel

One sunny day in October, when the leaves were turning a crisp golden brown, my sister and brother-in-law, Valerie and Mark, were readying to leave on a trip to California. They were heading south to help a friend in need, leaving behind their two teenage sons and their teenage daughter, along with two of their friends. Their mobile home was nestled among giant cottonwood trees.

Autumn in Boring, Oregon, a rural farm area near Portland, always seems to bring a gentle wind whispering through the trees. On this particular day, however, a sudden burst of wind whipped the branches of one of these cottonwood trees with great force.

Mark and Val's suitcases were packed and lined up at the door of the house, ready to be loaded into the family Suburban. While getting ready to depart, after noticing the unusual wind, Mark felt an urge to move the vehicles. Valerie stood at the door beside the suitcases and watched as he moved the cars in the driveway around. *What is he doing rearranging the cars when we need to finish loading so we can get on our way?* she thought.

But there he was, moving their green Suburban—the car used for hunting and camping trips—to the front of the driveway, and their daughter's junker, nicknamed La Bomba, towards the center of the driveway, near the corner of the house.

Last-minute instructions were given to the teenagers. As was their custom, Val and Mark gathered their children and friends around for a circle of prayer, all holding hands.

"Dear Lord," they prayed, "as we leave our home and our children behind in Your care, please send one of Your angels to watch over our home and children. Please keep them safe until our return. Amen."

After the prayer, Mark and Val finished packing and then headed to California. After all five teenagers went to bed late in the evening, the wind began to pick up. It blew so ferociously that it woke all of them around 3:00 in the morning. They become alarmed. The gusts of wind began ripping and tearing the tree limbs from the cottonwood trees as if they were toothpicks. The kids sat huddled together wondering what would come next.

CRAAAAAAASH! The horrendous noise sent chills along their spines. Startled, they jumped up, scrambled through the mobile home, and ran to the windows looking for signs of what had happened. The home was intact; nothing had been damaged. Feeling great relief, they slowly ventured outside. There, to their horror, was a huge cottonwood tree lying across La Bomba, the junker. They stared in amazement, mouths wide open. Still in her nightclothes, Heidi, my niece, walked over to where the tree had just been uprooted. There was a huge hole in the ground. The tree had fallen within inches of the front bedroom, where minutes ago the teenagers had been sleeping. The only casualty was Heidi's junk car. It was totally flattened.

Because of their prayers, God had set one of His guardian angels over them that night. As that mighty cottonwood tree began to fall, the angel must have reached out and given a gentle shove in order that the children inside the mobile home would be safe.

Stranger from the Sea

My little sister, Laura, and I were visiting our grand-parents' house at the beach in Lincoln City, along the Oregon coast. As small children, Laura and I loved to go down to the beach and build sand castles with our buck-ets and shovels. On one particular foggy Saturday morn-ing, my sister, about five years of age, and I were frolick-ing near the edge of the water. We were playing tag with the surf as the waves rolled up on the beach.

"Let's play 'Mr. Professor,'" I said as I spotted a log nearby. She quickly smiled in agreement, then ran and attempted to jump on the log. She quickly slid back down. The log was too big for her little arms to grab on and pull her up. I walked to where she lay in the sand and hoisted her on the log. She stood straight atop the log and adjust-ed her skirt.

"Now, Mr. Professor," she cooed, as if she were a grown up, "what are we going to learn about the ocean today?"

We quickly became enraptured by our game. As I would point to the ocean and describe where I thought the waves came from, she would giggle and ask yet another question.

As the tide came in, the waves quickly began lapping up to our log. After a few moments the tide began to swell and completely surrounded the log. Thinking we were beginning to be in danger, I told her to jump down and we would go back to the house. But just as she began low-ering herself, a huge wave crashed into the log and pulled it back into the ocean. She tried desperately to hang on with her little arms, but she was slipping into the water.

I began panicking. I looked up and down the beach, searching frantically and screaming for anyone to help. There was no one.

"Hang on, Laura!" I yelled as I began running to the stairs leading to our grandparents' house. I turned and saw the cold waves jostle the log ferociously up and down, pulling it further and further away from the beach. For a while, she continued to cling to the log with all of her might. Then she began to lose her grip, and I watched her slide down the side of the log. Devastated, I realized I might lose her and I quickly breathed a prayer as I continued running to the house.

Suddenly, a fisherman appeared from nowhere next to the log, and with the ocean tide breaking against his hip waders, quickly snatched Laura from it. Like carrying a baby in his arms, he hauled her out of the water and set her on the sandy beach.

Having heard my earlier screams, my parents and grandparents ran out of the house, down the steps, and on to the beach. We all ran towards Laura. Before we could get to where she stood crying, the fisherman had disappeared. When questioned about the incident, my sister and I could not remember seeing anyone on the beach before, nor were there boats offshore.

We have frequented that spot on the beach many times through the years and have yet to see anyone fishing there.

Forgiveness

I met Nancy when she was twenty-eight. As a young child, she had been repeatedly molested by her father. Years and years of therapy had followed, but to no avail. The nightmares, the bitterness, the hate, the frustration were foremost in her thoughts daily. "Why me?" she would scream into the night. "Why won't God strike that man dead? How could such a terrible thing happen to a child of three? Where was the justice?" These questions tormented her night and day. The idea of being victimized at such a young age held her captive to the point where her life became unbearable.

On her way home from work one day, Nancy noticed clouds forming. At first, rain began to fall lightly. She looked skyward and smiled as the drops began caressing her face. After a few moments, the rain began coming down harder. Then came the downpour. With no umbrella, she began running down the sidewalk looking for shelter. Across the street she spotted a building with its doors open. She quickly ran towards the double doors and ducked inside. She looked around and noticed it was a church. She slowly moved towards the front and sat down in one of the pews. As the sun began to peek through one of the stained-glass windows, the silhouette of the saint inlayed within it seemed to begin smiling down upon her.

For the first time in years, Nancy began to feel peace.

Noticing the woman in the pew, the pastor of the church walked down the aisle from the back of the building to greet her. His voice was soft as he extended his hand

and introduced himself. For a brief moment she hesitated. Her distrust of every man became obvious. Then she reluctantly took his outstretched hand.

Instantly, Nancy broke down. She blurted out the story of her life. She told about her father and how she was molested as a child. She told how she hated her mother for not coming to her defense and protecting her. Her sobs went on for what seemed an eternity. The pastor simply sat next to her, held her hand, and quietly listened.

Finally, when she seemed to have gotten it all out, the pastor spoke. "Yes, I understand your pain and your hurt. Yes, I understand that what your father did was horrible. Yes, I understand that your mother's silence has been unacceptable to you all of these years. But we must leave our pain and our bitterness with God. Only with Him can we find ultimate peace." The pastor paused as he thought of the words that he might use to help heal her spirit.

"Are you willing to forgive him? Are you willing to forgive your father for the anguish that he has caused you through all of these years?"

Nancy remained silent. She wiped the tears from her eyes. The agony of the thought of forgiving that man almost consumed her. She knew forgiving him would mean she would have to lay her lifetime of bitterness and resentment at the altar.

The man of God laid his hands upon her and prayed for the miracle of healing to enter her life. She closed her eyes. Tears continued to stream down her face. She squirmed as she struggled with the thought of forgiving her father.

Over the years, Nancy did find the courage to forgive her father. She learned, like so many others have, that forgiveness releases us from the bondage that we often place ourselves in when others sin against us. That heavy burden was lifted. She learned to live again and realized that even when man's love fails us, God's love remains sufficient for all our needs.

Chapter 8

―――――――▼―――――――

OUR FUTURE

God wants our future to be bright and peaceful. But we cannot have this bright future the way we are living now. If we continue on our current path, we will see an increase in fires, floods, hurricanes, and earthquakes—even in places where these disasters have not yet occurred—as manifestations of God's judgment on us.

Economic catastrophe, in the form of recessions, unemployment, or even a stock market crash, looms on our horizon as well.

On the other hand, technological advances promise to enhance our lives. For example, satellites placed into distance orbits with large solar arrays will gather and beam back sunlight to receiving stations in concentrated form, allowing a virtual endless supply of energy. Cars will come equipped with radios that will play one of your favorite songs with the push of a button. Unlimited access to entertainment media through the Internet will enable quick, interactive access to thousands upon thousands of songs, books, and movies. Any of these can be ordered from a list indexed by title, year, or artist, or even by a single word in the title.

On the environmental front, high-speed ships equipped with centrifugal separators will be called to areas where super tankers have run aground and are leaking oil into the ocean. These ships will quickly siphon the largest part of the oil spill and run the oil and water mix through machines, rapidly removing the oil from the water before it can reach shore or otherwise damage fish or wildlife. The remaining oil slick will be treated with natural oil-eating bacteria that will themselves be eaten by small fish or absorbed by plankton.

New structural procedures and stronger construction materials will result in larger and taller buildings. Japan's largest cities will be dotted with computer-controlled greenhouses on top of skyscrapers. These skyscrapers will recycle all water and waste and feed millions through the food grown in the greenhouses.

The entire Continent of Asia will feed her millions by building these greenhouse skyscrapers that amplify sunlight through the walls and roof and recycle water and nutrients. Every available cubic meter will be filled with hanging vegetables and newly discovered (genetically engineered) pods, beans and fruits.

Computer-controlled helicopters will carry small water hoses and platforms quickly up the sides of burning buildings, spraying water directly into the windows and rescuing people from the sides of these buildings rather than the tops, where smoke and flames are most concentrated.

The destroyer will replace the aircraft carrier as the fleet's flagship. As the battleship was replaced by the aircraft carrier in World War II, so the aircraft carrier will be replaced by the more efficient destroyer. With their long, barreled guns firing shells powered by linear motors, they will rapidly send five-inch shells hundreds of miles into terrorist base camps or into rogue nations. Brilliant missiles can be launched literally thousands of miles, destroying entire military installations or bunkers where weapons of mass destruction may be stored. Because of their rapid deployment, relatively low cost, and ability to keep their crews far from harm's way, these destroyers will become the newest and most potent weapon of anti-terrorism.

The following are other areas where I see dramatic change, both for good and for bad:

Information Management

Mini GPS (global positioning system) devices will be created, allowing us to search for anything small that is easily lost. Transmitters accessing this system will become smaller, enabling us to place them in wallets and on key chains. Handheld devices will allow us to find the distance and the direction by simply following a lighted arrow. The brighter the arrow, the closer we are to the object. Perhaps the best use of these systems will be to keep track of our small children—not to mention our teenagers—when we are at the mall.

More-efficient Vehicles

Vehicles will change drastically. Trucks will consume less fuel because their trailers will have electric motors in wheels powered by high-efficiency batteries stored underneath. The batteries will gain power from several sources, including solar panels located on top of the trailers and from "regenerative" braking as the trailer slows the truck down hills and brings the rig to a halt at stop signs.

Automobiles will have computer-controlled acceleration systems. When you're driving on slick roads or if you're taking a corner too fast, the computer will over take the car's braking and acceleration systems and will apply power or braking to the wheel that will best keep the car under control. This system will be especially useful in race cars, where rapid acceleration and control around corners is necessary. During acceleration, the computer will be able to detect which tire is spinning and will provide power to the other three wheels. If the race car is too close to other cars or a barrier, or if the system determines that the car may spin out of control around a corner, the computer will overcome the driver's throttle, brake and transmission settings and apply power or braking where needed to retain control.

Fifteen Minutes of Fame for Everyone

Thanks to improvements in Internet access, everyone will have opportunity for their 15 minutes of fame, as Andy Warhol predicted. Billions of people will have access to the Internet, and each user will be able to fine-tune their Internet software to the level of messages they wish to receive. Some of us will wish only to accept messages from those living within our cities or region, while others will be "wide-area enabled," allowing messages from a whole nation. We will be able to build databases of people, places and words that we do not want to receive. Those who wish to e-mail to potential billions may do so by simply clicking the Microsoft "blue world" icon located to the left of the Windows 2010 screen. Internet users all over the world who have no restrictions set on their e-mail will receive your message.

Increased Life Spans

Many new inventions will help increase our life spans and improve quality of life as well. Doctors will discover all of the necessary nutrients our bodies need (only a tiny portion of which has been discovered thus far) and will program our in-home computers with this vast array of knowledge. Computers will enable the quick and painless monitoring of our level of health. Each time we walk into our homes, for examples, our computers will inform us: "I would suggest you have a glass of orange juice because your level of vitamin C is low," or, "Jog up and down the stairs five times because your level of serotonin is too low." An entire snap shot of our health will be found through saliva and urine samples. By the year 2050, human life span beyond 100 years will become the norm.

New Views of Space

Multiple telescopes will be placed in orbit around earth, enabling stereoscopic views of galaxies millions, even billions, of light years away. These telescopes will be synchronized to allow clear, three-dimensional views of specific moons and asteroids orbiting other planets. Each telescope will contribute to the 3-D image by seeing the object from a slightly different angle.

A New Breed of Super Computers

Computers will be able to reprogram themselves and fix other computers. Machines with incredible speeds and capacities will allow larger amounts of data to be collected and stored, thus allowing our knowledge base to continue to increase exponentially. Currently, our knowledge base doubles every three to five years. Super computers will decrease this cycle to one year and even six months shortly in the 21st century!

By storing all known written, historical information into these computers, we will be able to cross-check stories for validity and, using newly developed algorithms, to successfully document accuracy of stories, including biblical ones. The speeds and memory capacities will allow highly complex programs that in turn will enable the computer to logically "think" like humans and fill in the missing historical pieces. Information about a historical figure, for instance, will be placed in a computer memory bank from all available printed sources. This data will then be summarized and put into logical, chronological order, while bits information that are contradicted by the majority of the information will be omitted.

Processing the enormous amounts of newly available information will create a new class of jobs. Highly technical people will be needed not just to process the information but also to understand it and interpret the data. Those who have first access to the data and can understand it may obtain great power. The most successful professionals of the next generation will be able to write programs that store, retrieve and process this enormous amount of data and make it available to the public in simple form. Some would say, "he who controls the internet has more power than a dictator".

The levels of education the general population will need to increase dramatically. People will have to become more technically literate just to understand how to input basic information into the computers we will use.

With these new high-speed computers, weather and climate will be predicted more accurately. Meteorologists will be able to input as much weather information as is known (generally from the past few hundred years) and will then predict weather patterns both for centuries to come and back to the beginning of the world's creation.

Relatively accurate models of the creation of both the universe and the animal kingdom will be extrapolated using these computers. In fact, scientists will be able to re-create the event of creation. The knowledge gained from this will surprise much of the scientific community. For example, it is currently believed that humans have existed on earth for more than a million years, yet there is no data to support this theory.

We will be surprised in finding how short a time man has lived on earth. Human populations will be mapped showing that population growth is exponential, not linear (unlike animals, humans have the capacity to reproduce no matter how harsh the environment). In prehistoric male-dominated societies, women were child bearers and had value placed upon them based upon the number of children they could have. So they started bearing children as soon as they were capable. Unlike today, population growth was necessary and held no ill effects. Children were needed as hunters-gatherers and to carry on the family name and legacy. We find no history written by humans before 12,000 B.C.

The entire human genome will be mapped. With these super computers, models that exactly mimic the replication of cells and DNA within living cells will be created. Down to the minutest detail, we will create living structures and attempt to accomplish the actual creation of living things in the laboratory from the basic building blocks of hydrogen, nitrogen, oxygen and carbon.

A "Bigger Brother"

Along with the positive potential of new inventions, there will be many ills. Government will place cameras on the street corners of every major intersection in the guise of enabling safer traffic and reducing crime. Instead, there will be a flood of tickets sent to scores of motorists as cameras snap pictures of the licenses of cars who fail to signal properly, decline to come to a complete stop before making a turn, or sail through yellow lights.

Tinier, more powerful—and less-detectable—cameras and listening devices will become the norm. Government agents will be able to monitor computer screens, watching people perform common daily functions and interacting with other family members. Taped conversations of interest to the government will be stored on super computers for generations.

Presidents of democracies will become more powerful and will hide more secrets from the public. More back-room deals will be made and "spin" will become a science as politicians learn how to read and manipulate public opinion polls.

Each of the 200 or more nations on earth will have fully developed nuclear technology, and most will spend much of their military budgets to improve those technologies. Individuals will be able to purchase bomb-making materials and order bio-chemical warfare materials online.

*   *   *   *

Military, economic, environmental, and entertainment inventions will abound. All that can be invented has not been invented, and so there is much to look forward to. But we must not forget God.

We need to relinquish our cynicism. We are doubting too much: we are doubting God and doubting ourselves. We must learn to exercise our faith.

There is still time to change. We must alter the way we are living. We are sinning against nature, against our neighbors, and against God. Yet we can still repent from our ways and return to our roots of faith, reason, and responsibility.

The gift of prophecy is a wonderful thing, yet it is more important to be able to shape the future than to predict it. This is what we must do—shape our futures.

We have a free will. Our destiny is determined by choice, not chance. We must invite God back into our lives and into our world. I believe that if we do change, with God, we can be saved from imminent doom.